1994

S0-BNB-672

The Hatchet's Blood

THE ANTHROPOLOGY OF FORM AND MEANING

Senior Editor
J. David Sapir (University of Virginia)

Associate Editors
Ellen B. Basso (University of Arizona)
J. Christopher Crocker (University of Virginia)
Hildred Geertz (Princeton University)
Peter A. Metcalf (University of Virginia)
Renato A. Rosaldo (Stanford University)

THE HATCHET'S BLOOD

~∞~

*Separation, Power, and Gender
in Ehing Social Life*

MARC R. SCHLOSS

The University of Arizona Press
Tucson

THE UNIVERSITY OF ARIZONA PRESS

Copyright © 1988
The Arizona Board of Regents
All Rights Reserved

This book was set in 10/12 Linotron 202 Bembo.
Manufactured in the U.S.A.

Library of Congress Cataloging-in-Publication Data

Schloss, Marc R.
The hatchet's blood.

(The Anthropology of form and meaning)
Bibliography: p.
Includes index.
1. Bayot (African People)   I. Title.   II. Series.
DT549.45.B39S35   1988   966'.3   88-1352
ISBN 0-8165-1042-3 (alk. paper)

British Library Cataloging in Publication data are available.

For Harriet and David

Contents

Preface

The Basse-Casamance region of southwestern Senegal, where the Ehing people live, is a strip of low-lying terrain that extends from the Gambia to the northern boundary of Guinea-Bissau. The region takes its name from the Casamance River which originates just east of the town of Kolda and winds its way 160 miles to the Atlantic. The Casamance is one of some two dozen waterways that cross the low plains of the Upper Guinea coast, a feature that once prompted Europeans to refer to the territory between Cape Verde and Cape Mount as "the Rivers of the South" (Rodney 1970: 2).

The country is a mixture of marshes, mangrove swamp, and low sandy plains covered with dense forests of palm. This terrain is the setting of a remarkable system of wet-rice agriculture. All the several peoples living there have claimed the low wetlands of the region where varieties of rice are thought to have been domesticated. As Linares (1981: 558) notes,

> The Casamance is postulated by Porteres (1962) to have formed part of an ancient heartland where indigenous varieties of the African rice species *Oryza glaberrima* were domesticated. Although Asian rice was brought to West Africa by Portuguese explorers in the early 16th

century, it did not reach the (Casamance peoples) until two centuries ago, supplanting the native species within the memory of living elders. By the time of the first European contact, the (Casamance peoples) and their relatives in what is now Guinea-Bissau had already converted much of the mangrove swamp fringing the tidal estuaries of important rivers into a network of paddy fields. . . . Indeed, they may have practised intensive agriculture on continuously cropped land for a thousand years or more.

In contrast to the shifting forms of agriculture chracteristic of much of Africa, where land is left to lie fallow, the peoples of the Casamance return year after year to the same paddy fields, to work the land they themselves have worked before, and to work the land known to their ancestors.

In Senegal today, the Basse-Casamance is known as the home of the Diola, a people of acephalous cultivators who may number close to 300,000. The Diola language is one section of the Bak branch of the West-Atlantic language family; the other branches are Manjak and Balanta (Sapir 1970), speakers of which are mainly found in Guinea-Bissau. His-torical and archaeological evidence suggests that the Diola themselves were once concentrated south of the Casamance delta, but, as a result of shifts of territory and migrations that began before the fifteenth century (Mark 1985, Linares 1981), they are now found in communities through-out the region, north to the Gambia and as far east as the Soungrougrou River. Although all Diola communities practice a way of life that suggests a common heritage, they are a congeries of peoples rather than a unified population. Diola are divided into at least ten dialect groups, and some of these are not mutually intelligible. Different communities also display a great deal of cultural and social variation.

The Ehing are one of the few peoples in the Casamance who are not Diola. With a population that runs to about 2,500, the people as a group are little known in Senegal. Those Senegalese in Dakar and even in Ziguinchor, the regional capital, who have heard their name (in Senegal, those who know of the people through French sources pronounce the name "Essing"), tend to identify Ehing as a Diola community, because their way of life is common to the Casamance. Though not surprising, this assumption is not accurate. Ehing belong to the same section of the West-Atlantic language family as the Diola, but their language and customs are distinct. Instead of the Diola, the Ehing may be grouped with their Senegalese neighbors, a people known as the Bayot (who call them-selves Kagere), and with the speakers of an Arame dialect who live in a village complex called Edii, about 20 kilometers south of the border in

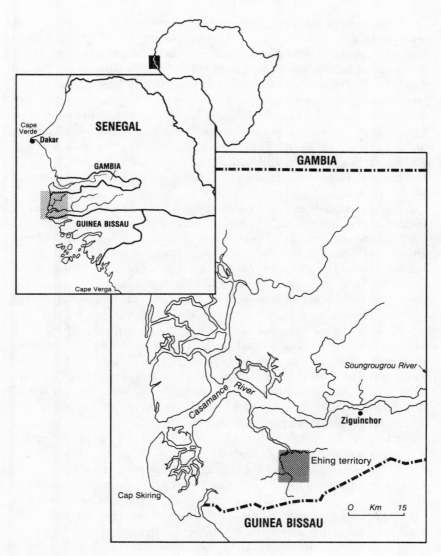

Lower Casamance.

Guinea-Bissau (Sapir, personal communication). The Ehing say they are especially close to the Edii; there is frequent traffic across the frontier and the groups share one cycle of initiation ritual.

In contrast to the extensive ethnographic and historical literature on the Diola,[1] very little has been directly written about these groups. Le

Prince provided a short description of the Bayot in 1905, and there are a number of references as well in Portuguese accounts (e.g., da Cunha Taborda, 1950). The Ehing have received even less documentation. There are scattered references to the "group Esigne" in Christian Roche's military history of the Casamance, where he suggests that Ehing territory was largely still unknown at the turn of this century. Despite their proximity to Ziguinchor, the Ehing and Bayot apparently were among the last groups in the region to enter into relations with the French (Roche 1976: 288). The area where the Ehing live remains one of the most forested landscapes in the region, and both forest and proximity to the southern frontier may have sheltered the people from early and extensive contact with Europeans.

Ehing territory lies to the south of the Casamance River, just east of the meander of Kamobeul. The land stretches from the meander of Nyassia, its northern boundary, toward the southern frontier with Guinea-Bissau. In all, their territory runs to about 130 square kilometers. The area is easily reached by a major route that runs from Ziguinchor through the southwest of the Casamance to Cap Skiring on the coast. At present the road is paved, although it was not at the time of my research when, during the rainy season, it was often impassable.

Ehing fall under the jurisdiction of the *sous-préfecture* of Nyassia. Nyassia is a Bayot village located on the main road about 8 kilometers to the northeast of Ehing villages. Nyassia is also the site of a Catholic mission and infirmary established in 1957. This infirmary, visited daily by both Bayot and Ehing, is a great resource in the area. The impact of Catholicism among the people, at least during the 1970s, was still minor. The effect of Islam, the predominant religion of Senegal, has been even more limited. Islam has had much greater impact and influence on the populations living north of the river.

The economy of the Ehing is singularly oriented toward two products: rice and palm wine. Rice, farmed with a hoe technology unique to the Casamance region, involves complex and cooperative forms of labor divided between men and women. For the other most important agricultural product, palm wine, Ehing harvest and ferment the sap of the oil palm—what they sometimes call its "blood"—to make wine. Tapping is exclusively the work of men, who climb the trees each morning and each evening to collect the sap in bottles. The season begins near the end of October, and in the months that follow an individual may tap twenty trees a day. During June and July the rains begin to dilute the sap and the season comes to an end for most of the villagers. But it is still possible to see, even in August, a few old men walking out to the groves with their baskets and climbing belts.

Drinking wine forms part of the daily round in Ehing life. Whenever men gather to sit and talk, a host brings out a bowl filled with the whitish wine. Using a small gourd with a stick attached as a handle, one dips in the bowl, drinks the wine in one long swallow, and passes the gourd around. Elders generally prefer to drink the stronger brew that has fermented at least several days; women typically prefer the sweeter wine fresh from the tree.

Wine is a traditional gift in Ehing society, and it plays a central role in marriage prestations. But its most important social use is in ritual. Whenever the people communicate with spirits, they offer wine, slowly libating from pitchers onto the shrines of spirits as they say their prayers and make their requests. Along with their Bayot neighbors, the Ehing have established something of a local reputation in the Casamance for the quality and quantity of their vintages. Several men in any village today transport their excess harvest to Ziguinchor, where it is sold to local merchants and tavern owners. The more industrious of these men may carry between 30 and 60 liters a week to town on their bicycles.

In addition to rice and wine, many villagers today cultivate manioc, and a very few farm groundnuts, an important cash crop in more northern areas of the region. The people keep various stock animals—cattle, chickens, pigs, and goats. These animals, especially cattle, are used in major ritual sacrifices. The meanders that border the villages offer fish, usually a small variety of carp. In some villages, especially those adjacent to the larger waterways, fish is an important component of the diet, but in other villages most meals may be plain rice, *kadia*. Many wild fruits are available in season. In any village a few individuals may hunt, but this is a minor activity, despite the fact that the dense woods still offer an abundant variety of birds, antelope, and monkeys. The dangerous animals, leopards and hippopotami, are no longer found in Ehingland, but there are many snakes, which are especially visible during the rains.

The peoples of the Casamance are acephalous. Entrenched in the marshes, waterways, and forests of the coast, they were in past centuries surrounded by, but not a part of, the Mandinka kingdoms of the Sudanic interior. Outsiders have repeatedly referred to communities in the region as anarchic and aggressive, peoples without rulers. Ehing villages do have chiefs, but this role was an innovation introduced during the Colonial era. It is not an indigenous institution, and chiefs do not exercise authority in the villages. One figure that has been referred to as a "king" in the Diola literature is *ai,* a ritual rather than political figure associated with the rains. The Ehing variant of this office is especially intriguing because the office is vacant more often than it is filled. Other positions of ritual authority are held by elders who are responsible for shrines that represent the many spirits that inhabit the Ehing world. This study takes its name and its subject from one such power, the most important and complex category in Ehing thought.

My fieldwork in Senegal was in three segments totaling twenty-two months. The period of research from December 1975 to May 1977 was supported through a grant from the National Institute of Mental Health. I returned to the field during the summer of 1978. In 1979, a grant from the Social Science Research Council enabled me to attend theEhing initiation. I thank these organizations for their generous support.

During my stay in Senegal, I was affiliated with l'Institut Fondamental d'Afrique Noire (I.F.A.N.). Abdoulaye B. Diop, then Chairman of the Department of Social Sciences and now the Director of the Institut, greatly facilitated my research and provided many kindnesses. Boubacar N'Diaye helped with many initial and final tasks in Dakar, and Abidou Sane did the same in Nyassia.

Many teachers and friends have contributed to this study. I would like to thank my teachers at the University of Virginia—Christopher Crocker, Roy Wagner, and Edward Winter—for their training and constant support. Olga Linares has always generously shared her knowledge of the Casamance with me and has, in many other ways, encouraged my work. I owe a special debt to my friend Charlie Piot, with whom I have discussed Ehing ethnography for countless hours. At various points, this book was read by Hildred Geertz and Ivan Karp, and I have benefited from their helpful and stimulating comments. I would also like to acknowledge here the help of Claudia Chang, Antonia Taylor, and my wife Harriet. Finally, there are two persons to whom I owe my deepest gratitude and thanks. Peter Metcalf worked tirelessly on this book, making creative and perceptive suggestions at every turn. I thank him here for his ideas, generosity, and editorial skills. To my teacher, David Sapir, I owe my greatest debt. He directed me to Senegal and has for many years been my intellectual guide and steady friend. Once before I thanked him for his patience that outlasted my confusion, and I now do so again.

There are very many Ehing whom I should thank here, but I cannot possibly mention all of their names. Throughout my stay in the field, I lived in Bakunum village, and I was received there with great warmth and patience. I owe my deepest gratitude to Mossi Bassene, Marie-Michele Tendeng, and Maxime Bassene for their friendship and constant help. They made what follows possible.

I am very grateful as well to the elders of all the villages. Ehing religion involves categories of knowledge and practice that are guarded from many members of their society. In the Ehing idiom, these forms of knowledge are taboo, *munyo*. *Munyo* involves separations between elders and youth, and especially between women and men. I owe more than I can say to those elders who allowed me to attend their rituals and who shared with me so much of their knowledge.

I have published some of this guarded material in this volume. In doing so, I do not betray a trust, for elders understood that I would write about their religion. But while I stayed among the Ehing, I kept the *munyo* to myself, and I remain committed to the practice that this knowledge not be related to anyone for whom it would be a breach of Ehing rules. Thus, if any readers of this book are persons for whom what follows is *munyo*, please read no further.

MARC R. SCHLOSS

The Hatchet's Blood

PART I

~~~

A Spirit's Domain

—how the central, essential red,
 escaped its large abstraction, became
 First, summer, then a lesser time,
 Then the sides of peaches, of dusky pears.
                          —Wallace Stevens

1

Odieng's Rules

The word *odieng,* in the language of the Ehing people of southern Senegal, means an ax or hatchet. A triangular blade of iron set into a wooden handle, the hatchet is used to prune palm trees and to split wood. In the past, before the introduction of steel machetes, men also used the hatchet to clear bush and hew timber.

This minor detail of vocabulary would be unimportant were it not for the larger significance of *odieng.* For, if one were to ask Ehing to specify what is essential to their way of life, they will first say wet-rice agriculture, and then, almost at once, they will point to a set of rules that are associated with a spirit (*esul*) also called Odieng.

Odieng as a spirit acts upon human beings almost in the same way that an ax acts on a tree. Infractions of the spirit's rules cause people to be struck with a condition the Ehing readily and graphically describe:

> When Odieng strikes, it is like fire. You see red, you see red with your eyes opened or closed. Your head pounds and pounds. The spirit has entered your body and drinks your blood.

No other spirit—and there are many other powers that inhabit this West African world—is so deadly.

Ehing are not in the habit of naming on any single and specific

3

occasion all of the rules of Odieng. Nevertheless, elders concluded, when prompted into discussion by my questions and cross-checking, that Odieng defined a set of eleven rules. These explicit and public prohibitions are known throughout each of the seven Ehing villages. And as a set, these rules are thought of as Odieng's "work," the work the spirit has performed since it came to dwell among the people.

In Ehing thought, two of the rules are felt to be the most important and are taken as the most serious offenses one might commit against the spirit. Appropriately, they are among the first rules I remember hearing. These rules are:

1. A man may not see a woman give birth.
2. A woman may not see Kombutsu, the ritual of initiation for male youth.

It is through these rules, and because of them, that one realizes that the separation of the sexes is a fundamental principle of Ehing social life.

In comparison with these two primary rules of gender separation, greater effort was required to discover and elicit the other rules of the spirit. There are two rules that concern menstruation:

3. Sexual intercourse is forbidden during menstruation.
4. Menstruating women may not go "up high"—that is, sit on stools or enter granaries.

The connection between these and the first rules may seem logical enough. These rules focus on issues of polluting substances, and a large literature in anthropology documents how ideas of pollution are often an aspect of the classification of male and female categories.

There are other rules of Odieng that refer to special prohibitions on the uninitiated, and it is these that begin to show the heterogeneous range of Odieng's activity:

5. Youth should not see a corpse.
6. Youth should have no prior knowledge of the initiation or of childbirth before their participation in these events.
7. Youth should not see human intestines.

The social category of "youth" (*ahula*) refers to any male who has not participated in the initiation and to any female who has not yet given birth. With the initiation and with first childbirth, youth become "elders" (*abia*), no matter what their chronological age. The rules applying to youth should not seem altogether puzzling, though perhaps the detail about intestines might seem odd. These rules focus on distinctions about status prior to the achievement of adult sexuality, and Odieng is a spirit that focuses on gender.

In a similar mode, Odieng regulates the life cycle with two other rules that require obligatory visits to the spirit's shrine:

8. After the initiation, youth must visit Odieng before emerging from ritual seclusion.
9. Before remarrying, a widow must visit Odieng on two separate occasions.

These rules form a parallel, in the sense the Odieng requires obligatory visits for men and women. But the circumstances stand in a curious sort of contrast, counterposing initiation and death along lines of gender.

And finally, there are two rules that most sharply give the set its complicated and heterogeneous character and that at first appear quite delphic:

10. Ehing may not see the rain-priest eat.
11. The people may not mix palm wine and water.

In defining and enforcing these prohibitions, Odieng again seems to be dealing with separation and classification. The tenth rule seems doubly extraordinary when it is realized that the office of rain-priest is often without an incumbent. To understand these rules, we need to know about the natural as well as the social order and, specifically, about the details and concrete practices of the agricultural cycle.

The aim of this ethnography is to work out why it is that these eleven rules—which, taken together, comprise a complicated and heterogeneous set—are felt by the Ehing to be so essential to their way of life. I shall argue that the spirit is so vital to the Ehing because its rules structure the entire system of production and reproduction that gives their life its form and its order.

Odieng and the Problem of Taboo

This book is about the sources and meanings of Odieng's power. To define these meanings, I draw on the ideas that several social anthropologists—Edmund Leach, T. O. Beidelman, and Mary Douglas—have put forward about the interpretation of ritual prohibitions. The general notion I am tracing is that rules of separation are a mode of classification.

Leach has suggested that taboos play a fundamental role in creating and marking distinctions in experience that is otherwise continuous and undifferentiated. In his view, language is the vehicle used to distinguish things in the world, a natural continuum; taboo is the vehicle that "inhibits the recognition of those parts of the continuum which separate the things" (1964: 157). Systems of cultural classification, in this argument, depend on and are reinforced by avoidances.

Beidelman likewise argues that prohibitions are basic to a study of classification. But he places less emphasis than does Leach on the cognitive features of interdiction—on why, as Leach says, "the foci of taboo fall where they do" (1982: 239). Instead, he has focused on how notions of separation relate to ambiguities in political life and, more to the point of this study, on how separations, and sometimes mixings of categories as well, are used to define and manipulate indigenous conceptions of power (Beidelman 1966, 1971).

Perhaps the most explicit statement on taboo, power, and classification is found in the work of Mary Douglas, especially in her monograph *Purity and Danger*. Douglas's argument rests on two fundamental ideas. The first is that taboos, as Leach has argued, are a way of marking off categories from each other, and, in this way, are a ritual means of creating cultural order. As Douglas (1966: 4) insists, the study of taboo belongs to an exploration of conceptual principles:

> ideas about separating, purifying, demarcating, and punishing have as their main function to impose system on an inherently untidy experience. It is only by exaggerating the difference between within and without, above and below, male and female, with and against, that a semblance of order is created.

This insistence on conceptual boundaries—and on the role of prohibition in the creation and maintenance of categories—is only the first step in Douglas's argument, but it is its foundation. In the second step, Douglas moves from general principles of classification to the particular meanings of rules in particular societies. It is not enough, she contends, to say that prohibitions establish categories and social definitions. The powers of a universe—such as the power of Odieng—ultimately refer to the social order. To put her case very directly, ritual separations rest on, and reflect, forms of social structure. She writes:

> All spiritual powers are part of the social system. They express it and provide institutions for manipulating it. This means that the power in the universe is ultimately hitched to society, since so many changes of fortune are set off by persons in one kind of social position or another. [Here she refers to the powers of witchcraft, sorcery, cursing.] But there are other dangers to be reckoned with, which persons may set

off knowingly or unknowingly. . . . These are pollution powers which inhere in the structure of ideas itself and which punish a symbolic breaking of that which should be joined or joining of that which should be separate. It follows from this that pollution is a type of danger which is not likely to occur except where the lines of structure, cosmic or social, are clearly defined.

Pollution, in brief, is a power "by which the structure is expected to protect itself" (Douglas 1966: 113).

In Douglas's argument, rules of separation are analogies of society; they encode points of danger and ambiguity in corporate and political life. Ritual dangers, in short, reflect social dangers. With this idea, Douglas tackles a number of concrete problems in the analysis of prohibition and purity.

No doubt her most celebrated example is that of the Jewish dietary laws, the Abominations of Leviticus. Douglas rejects the notion that these rules might be explained as allegories of vices or virtues, as utilitarian rules of hygiene, or as a meaningless and arbitrary set of proscriptions. Instead, she interprets the rules in terms of the "total structure of thought" (Douglas 1966: 41) that characterized Hebrew culture. Beginning with the observation that each of the rules is prefaced by the command to be holy, Douglas unpacks the meaning of the concept. Holiness involves notions of separateness, completeness, and wholeness. It also involves keeping distinct the categories of creation, the creation detailed in the Book of Genesis. The argument that follows is that the dietary rules "develop the metaphor of holiness on the same lines" (1966: 54).

In particular, she relates the distinction between clean and unclean animals to the classification of the world in the creation story—a division into earth, waters, and firmament. Then she makes her case (1966: 55):

> Leviticus takes up this scheme and allots to each element its proper kind of animal life. In the firmament two-legged fowls fly with wings. In the water scaly fish swim with fins. On the earth four-legged animals hop, jump, or walk. Any class of creatures which is not equipped for the right kind of locomotion in its element is contrary to holiness.

In this view, the dietary laws "would have been like signs which at every turn inspired meditation on the oneness, purity, and completeness of God" (1966: 57).

In this case, Douglas's interpretation—closely following the implications of the cosmology she is analyzing—turns almost totally on the concept of classification. She does little to develop the second phase of her own notion of taboo—that rules of separation and concepts of cosmic power and danger refer to social forms. But, in a later chapter in *Purity and Danger,* "The System at War With Itself," the link between taboo and social structure becomes much more explicit. Douglas attempts to link notions of sexual pollution to structural contradictions in social norms and practices. Among the Enga of New Guinea, for example, contact with women, when they are menstruating or during intercourse, can sicken a man, turn his blood "black," and eventually lead to death. Douglas traces this view of the dangers of menstruation to the marital structure of the Enga. In this competitive society, men seek women from clans who are traditional enemies. The pollution beliefs about women refer to their ambiguous position, as wives who are the sisters of enemies. And, "the contradiction which the Enga men try to overcome is the attempt to build marriage on enmity" (1966: 148).

Among the Lele of central Africa, to cite another of Douglas's cases, the social structure again embodies a contradiction but of a different sort. There the status of men is achieved through the control of rights over women. Yet this principle runs against a set of conventions that allow women opportunity and resources to play individual men off against each other. Lele women, as Douglas characterizes them, are not only active pawns; they are active intriguers. Here "individual men were right to fear that individual women could spoil their plans, and fears of the dangers of sex only too accurately reflect its working in their social structure" (1966: 152). Again, "the particular dangers which female contact threatens to males express the contradiction of trying to use women as currency without reducing them to slavery" (1966: 152).

In each of these cases, Douglas seems to suggest a double relationship between rituals about sexuality and the structure of society. The rituals and notions of pollution are, first of all, representations of the social tension: symbolic dangers refer to social dangers. Relationships of power, vulnerability, and tension are metaphorically encoded in pollution beliefs. And second, the ritual avoidances and washings found in a society are ways that try not only to express but to "handle" social contradictions. If relations with women are the palpable source of a contradiction, an attempt is made to deal with the contradiction by rituals and rules that prohibit contact with the source of the social difficulties.

Douglas's arguments about taboo are very suggestive for a study of Odieng. Like the Hebraic Abominations, the spirit defines a series of rules that must not be taken in a piecemeal fashion, for they too make sense only as part of a "systematic ordering of ideas" (1966: 41). And likewise, Odieng must be seen not only in terms of classification but in terms of a

social world. And, more to the point, that social world involves contradiction and structural tension, especially about gender.

Following Douglas, I too try to locate the power of Odieng in
society: this is a major premise of my study. But as any ethnography
makes it own demands, I do not apply her notion of the correspondence
between cosmos and society mechanically.[1] There is a fundamental difference in the way I have developed her tools for the study of taboo. Rather
than argue that Odieng's rules either express or preserve a social structure,
I emphasize the ways in which prohibitions actually organize social experience. Ritual dangers in the Ehing world are not ways to encode social
dangers; they are ways in which social rights and categories are positively
defined.

In the most sparse terms, the concrete questions that I try to resolve in
my interpretation are these: why does Odieng exclude women from the
initiation, and why men from birth? This problem of sexual separation
structures all the details of Ehing life that follow. The point I will demonstrate is that these two prohibitions embody a structural tension between
the sexes. There is a veritable contest in Ehing thought about the powers
that belong to men and women—and about the social rights that are
thought to devolve from these powers.

The first part of my interpretation, "The House," works through the
problem of the initiation. The "House" (*edop*) is a key concept in Ehing
thought because it refers both to a physical dwelling and a category of
descent. It is a concept that links descent to the work of men, who build
houses, and one that links descent, in turn, to the ideas Ehing hold about
land.

To understand Odieng's rule about the initiation, I need to explore the
concept of the House in detail. I especially need to show how this concept
is implicated in Ehing ideas about reproduction. The notion of a House
rests on a conception of souls that make up the membership of a descent
group by cycling through the generations. The souls pass from persons to
the land which belongs to a House, and from that land back to members
of the descent group. This cycle is a fundamental conception of Ehing
culture, and a primary theme of the initiation.

I explore these ideas about souls, descent, and men by organizing the
discussion around one of the few myths Ehing recounted during my stay
among them. It is a story about a primordial marriage, a tale that explicitly sets up the theme of the structural tension between the sexes. In
the text, a man and a woman contest where they are to live. The problem
is resolved when, finally, the man builds a house into which the woman
must move. The whole story serves as an indigenous piece of social

theory. In point of fact, a woman must move in marriage into the man's residence because of the cycle of souls: the building of a house and the locality of men emerge as the idioms through which Ehing construct the principle of descent.

In the initiation, a ritual that takes place directly under the auspices of Odieng, these ideas about descent find their most forceful expression. In entering the forest to cut themselves in a circumcision, men bleed in the same place as did their fathers. Land and blood are combined in a single image, an image that parallels the notion of a cycle of souls. But the initiation, as the rules of Odieng make clear, is a complex depiction of male powers. The rules reveal that, when men bleed, they appropriate to themselves the signs of female fertility and realize their powers to create a line of descent over and against the powers of women. This message is what makes the initiation so important.

In the second part of my interpretation, "Rain, Rice, and Land," I work, as the focus of my argument, toward an understanding of the reciprocal rule that forbids a man from seeing a birth. In other words, I explore the structural tension between the sexes from the other side of the equation. Curiously, the explanation of this taboo rests not in a discussion of reproduction itself, but in the technicalities of production. Odieng, I will argue, defines the powers and rights of women, and, to make sense of this part of the spirit's work, I need to describe the role of women in the economy. The labor of women is crucial in rice production, a point emphasized by the fact that women hold rights to their own granaries and to their own land. Rice emerges as a symbol of female labor in a system of social and symbolic classification, and this conception of labor is coterminous with the rules of separation that Odieng defines.

The key rules of the spirit give meaning to the rights that constitute the Ehing division of labor. This is a core point I develop through the exploration of Odieng's work; from this point I investigate, and account for, all the rules of the spirit—from those that focus on gender to those that relate to the natural order. In this way I show that Ehing prohibitions do more than reflect social dangers or handle social contradictions. I demonstrate instead that these prohibitions order the ideas and the tensions that inhere in productive and reproductive activities.

Odieng and the Problem of Land

This book is a study in symbolic classification, in the meaning of Ehing notions of separation. But it also aims to make a second comparative contribution to African studies. By closely analyzing the principal categories of Ehing society, I hope to be able to deal with an anomaly in social structure that would have perplexed ethnographers of the last generation.

Various formal features comprise a general image of West African descent systems, an image based on classic studies such as those of the Tallensi and the Tiv. The systems are patrilineal and patrilocal: the local community is composed of a localized patrilineage. Among the Tiv, for example, the compounds of the descendants of an ancestor form a discrete territorial bloc called a *tar* (Bohannan and Bohannan 1953: 20). The Tallensi—in their development of the connection between descent and locality—hold that some descendants of a lineage founder should always live on ancestral land, where shrines devoted to these ancestors are located (Fortes 1945, 1949). Lineages are property-holding corporations, and land, lineage, and shrines analytically belong to one conceptual scheme.

Now such a stereotype of West African descent entirely characterizes Ehing society. In fact, in some ways the Ehing seem even more lineal than the classic examples. The people live on their ancestral land, and they may have done so for centuries. Lineages are explicitly defined, through a system of shrines, as land-holding corporations. More than that, the land itself is identified with the past and future of the lineage. For to the Ehing, land is the home of their souls. In their thought, ancestors are reborn as children through the generations as souls cycle from persons to land in a cycle of reincarnation. Land is both a resource for production and a vehicle of reproduction. Land is descent.

And yet, women inherit land. Not only do they hold rights to land, they also keep their own independent stores of rice in their granaries. Access to these granaries is governed by strict rules of constraint: neither husband nor wife can enter—or even look into—the other's granary without permission. In a comparative context and, perhaps more to the point, also in a context of Ehing ideas about descent and land, these practices, especially the norms of land inheritance, seem puzzling, even contradictory. How are they to be understood?

I shall argue that this situation is a result of the same ideas about production, reproduction, and gender that we are led to explore in an analysis of Odieng. My strategy is to demonstrate that symbolic anthropology can deal with problems in social structure in a manner that goes beyond the range of the classic approaches in African ethnography that are governed by a more narrowly social or legalistic perspective.

2

Odieng's Ritual

Ehing claim to experience Odieng in two ways. They encounter the spirit, most acutely, when it "catches" them and makes them ill. And they encounter Odieng in ritual, when they communicate with the spirit at its shrines. In much of this ritual, elders seek to treat the sick by asking Odieng to "let go" of the person who has broken its rules. On other infrequent occasions, elders libate wine at the shrine to plan for, and announce, Kombutsu, the initiation which the spirit governs.

In later chapters, my focus will be on the conditions that are thought to provoke Odieng into activity—the eleven rules the spirit defines. But before I take up the question of the meaning of these prohibitions, I begin by placing Odieng in its social world.

A Land of Houses and Spirits

The Ehing believe they are the first people to occupy their territory. Their oral history recounts that they came originally from a large village called Iribun, located to the south in what is now Guinea-Bissau, in search of land suitable for growing rice. Finding valleys where the terrain was relatively open, the people dispersed to claim and clear the land and they settled into villages. In this story, as sparely as it is told, the Ehing link the definition of themselves as a people to their mode of subsistence, and it is a link that is echoed in their vocabulary; the verb "to clear land" also means "to be present."

Several groups in the Casamance make similar statements about a movement from the south, and these may accurately reflect past migrations. But it is important to realize that what Ehing say may refer to a very distant past. Paul Pélissier has suggested that the area south of the river, which includes the Ehing zone, was the earliest area inhabited in the region (1966: 663), and archaeological work just east of the Kamobeul meander puts occupation at A.D. 200. (Linares 1971: 48). Although there is yet to be any dating for the Ehing themselves, it is quite possible they have been in their present location for many centuries.

At present the population is divided among eight villages: Dioher (about 400 inhabitants), Bafikan (390), Bakunum (340), Dialang (310), Kalian (235), Kuring (160), Etafun (120), and Nyame (whose inhabitants the census numbered into the population of Bakunum). The villages lie on a continuous plateau covered with thick forests of palm and patches of savannah (see Fig. 2.1). This upland area is more or less surrounded by lower valleys where the terrain has been converted into rice fields, and these fields in turn border mangrove swamp and meanders. Paths crisscross the plateau to connect the villages; at most the villages lie about an hour's walk from each other.

Although villages are a named, spatial category, they are not directly implicated in claims to land. Rather, all the land in Ehing territory is divided among patrilineal categories that are called Houses. In the Ehing view of their settlement, the original immigrants from Iribun claimed both upland regions of the plateau and low-lying valleys, and since that time rights to the land have passed in a male line to their descendants.

When I did my fieldwork, I counted some forty Houses among the different villages. The more populous villages were composed of up to eight Houses, and the smallest villages of two or three of these groups. The members of a House—the male members, since it is the men who build houses—live together in local groups, which are often set apart from each other along the edge of the upland, overlooking the rice fields. In the more expansive villages, it is a good ten- or fifteen-minute walk between these groups, on narrow paths that wind through dense groves of palm and thick bush. In other, more nucleated villages, the distance between courtyards is much less; groups are separated by a hundred yards or so.

A House (lineage) is a central social concept that Ehing use to organize themselves, and Houses can be readily described as corporate

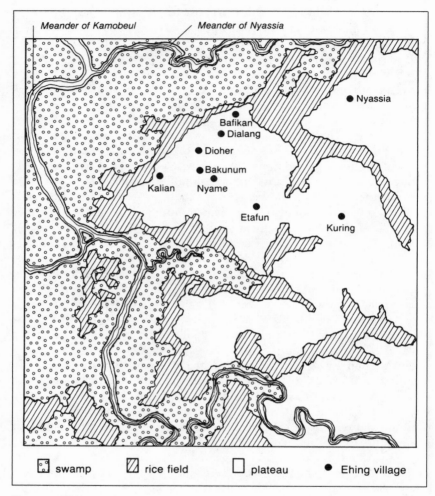

Fig. 2.1. Ehing territory.

groups. Apart from these groups, the society is also divided into patronymic categories (*obuo*), which, in the literature on the Diola, have sometimes been referred to as clans. There are, at present, six patronyms in
the population: Nyafouna, Bassene (Manga), Batiga, Sagna, Tendeng,
and Famara. Ehing claim that Nyafouna, Batiga, Bassene, and Sagna are
traditional names, but some of these are found among Diola groups as
well. Tendeng, they recount, are immigrants from the neighboring
Bayot, where they are much more populous. The name Famara, perhaps

of Wolof origin, was adopted by a single lineage in Bafikan village during the lifetime of living elders.

These patronymic categories are exogamous, but, unlike lineages, they do not have founding ancestors. Some categories, however, are associated with shrines where people gather once or twice a year. Names are also associated with particular animal categories.

Not every name category is represented in every village. Dioher village, for example, has lineages that belong to the Nyafouna, Bassene, Tendeng, and Sagna categories; and Nyame has two Houses, one of Sagna and one of Bassene. Furthermore, some villages, like Bafikan, contain several lineages bearing the same patronym.

This, then, is a rough description of the social world in which Ehing encounter their spirits. Having described briefly the social terrain, I will now sketch the contours of the cosmos.

Ehing possess no mythology about the creation of their physical world; there is no narrative in which earth and sky, the meanders and the forest, are given foundation. Perhaps this lack of interest in natural origins reflects the ideology the people hold about their immigration from the south; their social life, in its present circumstances, begins in a world that is already created. In contrast to people like the Dogon of Mali (Griaule 1965), whose spectacular cosmology seems to encompass the most minor details of everyday life, the Ehing initially impress one as practical farmers, with their heads turned toward the soil.

The one category that, in a logical sense, stands at the beginning of the world is the concept of Iri. In some contexts, this word might be translated as God, but this must remain a loose and rather problematic translation. For Iri also means, in various contexts, year, sky, and rain.[1] The concept of Iri as God, it would seem, is always infused with images of the natural cycle; for a year is composed of the rain and dry seasons, of dark and bright skies, of the time of working the rice fields and the time of wine, ritual, and village activities.

Ehing feel that Iri figures importantly in their lives, though the concept is in no sense analogous to our concept of a personal god. When pressed, they might acknowledge Iri as the creator of the world, but this concept is best understood in the sense that Iri, as rain and as an embodiment of the natural cycle, underwrites all experience. Iri is the condition of and the source of human productive activity, but it is not a concept bound up directly in human affairs.

Instead, the figures that Ehing deal with most immediately in their experience are the various powers they know as *esul,* a term I shall translate as spirits. Most spirits make their presence known to the people through the illnesses and other misfortunes they are thought to bring, and much of Ehing ritual is directed toward these figures—either to ask for help in some form or, more frequently, to ask the spirits to "let go" of anyone they have "caught."

Ehing recognize different kinds of figures among their spiritual powers. There are spirits that they believe are indigenous to their culture, and there are other spirits that have been "imported" from neighboring peoples. The number of major indigenous spirits is quite limited. Apart from Odieng, there are the spirits Kahin, Echin, Baliga, Kaba, Kahus, Kai, and Teno and it is these that receive attention in this study. The large number of imported spirits play a less pervasive role in social life. They have been brought from other regions of the Casamance, by ritually importing the soil from another area, to accomplish a particular purpose: in one man's house, to guard against a rash of illness; in another man's fields, to watch against those who would spoil his crop.

Ehing communicate with all of the spirits they know at shrines. There the people offer libations of palm wine or sacrifices of animals, and there they make their requests and their confessions. Authority over shrines is held by the elders of the Houses on whose land the shrines are located.

The shrines themselves are quite simple. Some spirits are represented by a forked stick of wood stuck in the earth, and others by nothing other than a hole in the ground. A few shrines are more elaborate: sticks or holes are covered with a small thatched roof. When not in use, shrines are often overgrown with weeds. Looking at some of the half-rotted pieces of wood, one would hardly suspect that this is the stuff out of which a cosmos has been made.

The major spirits are each represented by several shrines. To state this more precisely, there are representations of some of the powers in each of the villages. Each village, for example, possesses a shrine of Echin, a spirit that afflicts persons who argue over rice. Likewise, each village houses a shrine of Kahus, associated with the initiation, and Baliga, a spirit involved with problems of infertility. In fact, Ehing sometimes define a village as the social unit that contains the shrines of these three powers.

In contrast to the representations associated with indigenous powers, "imported" spirits are usually figured through a single shrine. This mode of representation suggests the more narrow range of their activity and importance. The exception to this pattern is Odieng. There are three shrines dedicated to the Hatchet, and these are all located on the land of two lineages, near the border that lies between the villages of Nyame and Bakunum. All Ehing, no matter what their village of residence, must walk to these sites when the Hatchet manifests itself.

In the previous chapter, I outlined the rules that Odieng defines. In this chapter, having sketched the social parameters of Ehing organization, I turn to the ritual through which the people communicate with this power.

Odieng's Affliction

When Odieng is thought to strike, its presence is recognized by a particular mode of illness. The first sign or symptom is a painful headache. The pain usually begins about dusk, lasts into the night, and is often accompanied by a feeling of faintness. By the next morning the headache has usually disappeared, but it begins again with dusk. Now among the Ehing, these symptoms are common enough; people frequently complain of headaches that have nothing at all to do with spirits. What clinches the diagnosis of Odieng is the report of seeing only red. The sick see red with eyes opened or closed, everywhere and at all times. Odieng, elders explain, causes this phenomenon by "taking your blood and putting it in your face." Odieng is "like fire." The spirit has "entered the body to drink blood."[2]

That a spirit might "catch" or "seize" someone is a common idiom in African thought. It is an idiom in which exterior forces are seen as the grounds of affliction, and it is one that is supported by the incontrovertible evidence of the illness itself. The Ehing variant of this theme is expressed by the verb *kalom*. *Kalom* is to catch something, to take hold of it. It is used to describe taking hold of someone's arm or picking up a piece of wood. But when spirits catch someone, they do not necessarily take hold of a person from the outside. Though spirits are exterior forces, they can somehow get inside a person to do their damage. The people were very vague about, and seemed to show little interest in, how this process works. I have heard them say that a spirit may come as does the wind and also that it catches as if it had a thirst, for "why else would we give it wine when we ask it to let go?" Ehing are decidedly less interested in a doctrine about the nature of spirits then they are in how to avoid their intrusions—and how, once not avoided, these intrusions can be remedied.

Ehing believe that any breach of Odieng's rules will lead to affliction. But they do not hold that the activity of the spirit is mechanical. Rather, Odieng is conceived in moral terms. Odieng is thought to judge, to take intention into account, and to work its power accordingly. This view of the spirit as a moral agent influences the circumstances in which people seek out the remedy of ritual.

In many cases these rituals will be held whenever someone realizes he or she has broken a rule, even before any symptoms of illness appear. As girls who have not married often take care of sick younger siblings, they sometimes will witness a death; immediately they confess to the spirit the circumstances. Youth, on their journeys to the cities and elsewhere outside of Ehingland, often inadvertently break a taboo of Odieng, and they will visit the shrine on their return to the village. I was told, for example, of instances when scenes in movies produced such confessions. There was also the case of a student who, after studying biology in high school in Ziguinchor, told the spirit that he had learned something about how women give birth. In this instance, shortly after class he developed a headache and took this as the first sign of Odieng's appearance.

I gained the impression that youth visited the spirit more readily than elders. Elders, I was told repeatedly, are often reluctant to admit they have broken a rule, even if the breach were not intentional. There is a sense of shame or embarrassment involved in these circumstances. Consequently, some individuals, having broken a taboo, nevertheless adopt a wait-and-see attitude, for there is always the possibility in Ehing thought that Odieng, as a moral agent, will sense contrition and ignore the violation. But the implications that follow from this understanding of Odieng cut both ways. Just as the spirit is thought capable of ignoring accidents, it is thought to condemn utterly volitional behavior. Should an elder intentionally violate a taboo, the ritual confession at the shrine would not prove efficacious. Odieng would not "hear" it.

The Ritual

To treat an affliction or to prevent one is, as the people say, "to walk on the path," the narrow path that leads to one of the shrines where a confession can take place. The ritual described below occurred at the shrine which lies behind the house of Sisa Sagna, an elder of Ta lineage. He, with his lineage brother Samaila, who lives about 50 yards away, are the two officiants responsible for regulating relations with the spirit.

Sisa performs the greater part of the ritual and administers to the patients; Samaila sits at the "head" of the shrine—that is, next to the hole in the ground which represents Odieng. The shrine itself is set within an elevated mound of earth which is covered with a thatched roof. Though the roof stands about 7 feet above the ground, the space within is not high enough for a man to stand. The mound is surrounded by a circular mud wall which reaches about halfway toward the thatch. At one end, the end facing away from Sisa's house, an opening has been left as a doorway into the shrine, and several small steps run from the sill to the ground.

When people come to the spirit, they bring with them a gourd of wine and a chicken the same sex as themselves. In addition, women patients must bring with them some pounded rice. I was told that women must bring the rice as a supplemental offering because the wine which they will use in the ceremony is not a product of their own labors. Since men themselves produced the wine which they bring to a confession, they need not make any further contribution.

The purpose of the ritual is to "cast off taboos" (*kahusen munyo*) and to ask Odieng to "let go" (*kaharen*) of the person who is "caught" (*kalom*). The ritual begins when Samaila goes inside the hut to sit at the "head," and Sisa positions himself on the top step, sitting with his back to the shrine. In the ritual I am describing, the patient is a middle-aged woman. She approaches the shrine and sits down on a step below Sisa with her back to him. She immediately hands him the wine and rice but for the moment holds onto the chicken. Both she and the elders are stripped to the waist, as the people always are whenever they communicate with any spirit.

Sisa begins the rite by placing an empty libation pitcher on top of the woman's head. The woman states the interdiction which has been broken, and hers is a complex and somewhat atypical case. This is her second visit to Odieng. During her initial confession she started to menstruate. Because she was menstruating at the same time that she was "up high" on the step, she was breaking a rule even as she asked for pardon. So she remained ill.[3]

Sisa takes the gourd of wine the patient has brought and pours a little wine into a small, broken clay pot (*dili*) which is kept at the shrine. The wine which remains in the gourd is emptied into a libation pitcher. Sisa then sharpens a small knife, also kept at the shrine, by rubbing the blade across the wood of the top step, and proceeds to cut the throat of the chicken which has been handed to him. The chicken is killed within the hut but not over the hole which represents Odieng. Sisa rubs the knife several times over the dead bird and makes an esoteric invocation. He holds the fowl over the broken clay pot so that blood falls and mixes with the wine.

Sisa then passes the pot to the patient who drinks the mixture. Next, Sisa picks up the libation pitcher, filled with wine only, takes some in his mouth, and spits it out onto the back of the patient. Sisa passes the pitcher back to Samaila at the head of the shrine. Sisa places his hands on the patient's shoulders and begins to address Odieng and sometimes "God" (Iri). As Sisa speaks, Samaila repeats the words as he libates wine onto the shrine.

> You have heard her speech. She told you how tired she is. She already came here once. She told you when she came here [i.e., she related the original taboo during the first confession]. She is sitting here on the step; Iri [here God and Odieng are conflated] caught her. She has spoken about her head that hurts. Also, as she knows nothing [her action was not intentional], and we have caught her here, let go so that her body becomes well. She didn't pay attention. Pardon [kwos] the taboo. Pity her body. Her body is still vital [active, otherwise well]. The work has arrived [work in the rice fields, it is July]. When she goes to her work, let her body be active. Pardon her as she came here today. Her chicken is here, which she brought. Her wine is here. We will leave her, she didn't mean it. We will go home to the rice fields, we won't eat something dirty.

After the speech and libation of wine, Sisa blows into the left ear of the patient and then into the right. He instructs the patient to walk away without looking back at the shrine. A man would walk out of the immediate vicinity of the shrine, where he would wash his feet. Women traditionally walk out to a pond in the rice fields, where they wash their entire bodies.

As the woman walks away, Sisa spills a few grains of rice, which the patient brought, over the spot where he killed the fowl. He keeps the rest, and he, Samaila, and other elders of his lineage will later prepare a meal. The elders at once drink any wine left after the libation.

The ritual results in Odieng's departure and cures the patient. Our task is to interpret the symbolic action that modifies experience. It is helpful to begin with an idea expressed in Sisa's speech. During that speech, Sisa appears to identify with the spirit ("we will let her go"), and this identification corresponds to his role as an intermediary between person and spirit. Although Sisa, as officiant, addresses the spirit on the patient's behalf, he hears the case along with the spirit in the sense that, when a patient comes to confess, Sisa must make an implicit decision whether to perform the ritual and therefore allow a confession. He is thus not only an intermediary but also a judge, and the ritual itself is referred to as a "judgment." In this connection, I was once told that "Odieng takes on the character of the elder responsible for it," implying that the pardon of the spirit is linked to the pardon of its elder. An unsympathetic elder would color the relationship between people and spirit. Though I never heard of a situation when an elder refused to perform a rite, Ehing are aware of his prerogative. For example, Sisa told me that he himself would be afraid to intervene on behalf of an adult who violated a taboo intentionally; were he to do so, Sisa remarked, Odieng might well attack him. It is noteworthy that Sisa repeats several times in his speech that the patient did something which "she did not know."

Once Sisa positions the empty libation pitcher, the patient offers the confession. As he once told me, the pitcher is the signal for the victim to speak. By verbalizing the interdictions she has committed, the woman "casts off" the *munyo* which provoked Odieng. Watching the symbolic action, it looks very much as if the empty pitcher were being filled with the taboo, as if the interdiction itself were corporeal and had to be removed to another space. The ritual makes clear, however, that this dissociation of interdictions and person is only one aspect of the cure. In Ehing thought, the patient has lost blood and thus suffers from an internal disorder. Though the confession provides a separation from the taboos, it does not in itself redress this internal distress.

Rather, order is restored through drinking the fowl's blood. This may be the act in the ritual whose meaning is least apparent, but several details point to this interpretation. The fowl brought to the "judgment" is always the same sex as the patient, for its blood must serve as a symbolic substitution for that of the person. Though the patient brings the fowl, the elder kills it and significantly does not offer the blood to the spirit. Because the elder gives the blood to the patient rather than the spirit, the ritual reverses the direction of the flow of blood which has characterized the affliction. It is as if the elder, acting for Odieng, is returning the blood the spirit has taken. This restoration of internal disorder is then marked by spitting wine on the patient's back; the contrast—blood and wine inside the body/wine outside—expresses the idea of blood back in its proper place and marks the transposition of taboos and blood. Sisa once commented, as an indirect corroboration of this interpretation, that if he were to spit blood and wine on the patient's back (which has never occurred), it would signal that the patient was going to die.[4]

After the reversal of blood, the priest asks the spirit's pardon, and only now does Odieng unequivocally receive an offering. As the spirit is given wine, Odieng is exhorted to no longer eat blood, to "let go" of the person.

The key to understanding this offering lies in the phrase "we won't eat something dirty." This is a highly condensed statement. Odieng is a spirit which consumes blood, and in Ehing thought this act is justified when someone has broken its rules. For the spirit to drink blood in this circumstance is not at all to eat something "dirty." Odieng is acting morally. The implication in the elder's exhortation, then, is that the ritual is altering the moral relationship between spirit and patient. This alteration is accomplished through two means: it begins with the confession, with its denial of intention and sense of contrition, and ends, simultaneously with Sisa's speech, with the offering of wine. With the offering, the spirit is thought to be under a reciprocal obligation to "let go" and cease its intrusion. To continue after receiving a gift would certainly then be to "eat something dirty," for the patient's blood, in a moral sense, no longer belongs to the spirit.

As the people say, and this reference is to relations between persons as well as between persons and spirits, "you don't eat the good of someone you are against." The acceptance of a gift confers an obligation to respond in kind. Just as it would be wrong for a curer to accept a payment for a patient he knows will not recover, it would be wrong for a spirit to receive wine and then still drink blood. It would be "to eat something twice," and that contravenes a proper moral relationship.[5]

Sisa, then, is reminding Odieng of the principles of moral interaction; he tells the spirit to go to the rice fields instead of remaining with the woman. It may also be noted that, since the interdictions have been associated metonymically with the libation pitcher, perhaps they also, with the wine, are symbolically returned to their guardian during the libation.

After Odieng receives the wine, Sisa blows in the patient's ear because, as he once told me, "Odieng has made her deaf." I should add, however, that blowing in ears is performed at the end of various ceremonies. The same action, for example, occurs when a curer finds an individual's lost soul and replaces it in his body.

As the patient leaves, she is instructed not to look back at the shrine, and this prohibition of sight reveals an underlying connection between the ritual and the taboos governed by the spirit. Several of the taboos—seeing birth, initiation, the "king," or a cadaver—center on prohibitions of sight. Others center on knowledge or contact which are figurative extensions of sight—preknowledge of birth or of initiation, or contact with menstruating women. The instruction not to look back appears in this context, therefore, as a reversal of what produced the affliction; the taboos are left behind and what was seen is to be seen no longer. In the Ehing idiom, what was "uncovered" has been re-covered.

Along with the correspondence of sight in the taboos and ritual, and just as important, is a correspondence of blood. This correspondence allows an observer to isolate one of the internal principles or devices of Odieng's symbolism. Several of the taboos (those which separate the sexes) focus on blood loss associated with sexuality. And since someone who violates these will be caught with an affliction which itself is defined as blood loss, we can see that Odieng produces in the transgressor himself (loss of blood) what he was to avoid (sexual bleeding). There is a symbolic transference of blood loss from one person to another which is rendered and given form in a representation of spirit. Further, once the forbidden bleeding is seen, the transgressor internalizes the tabooed image: he constantly sees "red." Thus, the transference operates visually as well as organically.[6] This is how the symbolism of Odieng works.

The Shrines of Odieng

There are three shrines that represent Odieng. Two of the shrines are set on land that formally belongs to Ta lineage in the village of Nyame. One is the shrine at Sisa's house, and the other, which lies deep in the woods and close to the border between Nyame and Bakunum, is a shrine reserved for rites that begin and end Kombutsu, the initiation. Access to this shrine, which I shall call the grand Odieng, is forbidden to women and youth. The third shrine is located on land belonging to Karaguba lineage. This shrine, like that at Sisa's house, is used for ritual confessions. But unlike Sisa's shrine, Karaguba's lacks a thatched roof: it is simply a hole that lies next to a large tree.

There is a myth that tells of the origin of the two shrines used in the curing rituals. In the story a man from Karaguba lineage found the spirit where the shrine for the initiation is now located. The spirit explained its work to the man, and the latter decided to take Odieng back to his home, carrying the spirit in a bundle of leaves. But on his way, he stopped at the home of his brother-in-law at Nyame. There he drank much wine and, because of his drunkenness, forgot to take the spirit with him when he continued toward home. Waking from a dream, Karaguba rushed back to Nyame, but it was too late: the spirit was already installed in the ground. And so, he returned to the original location in the woods where the spirit gave him another shrine.

Though a shrine remains today on Karaguba's land, the lineage itself is no longer responsible for its ritual. Karaguba is a lineage that has suffered the loss of all its adult men. Authority over the shrine has therefore passed to the men of Kabe lineage, who live in Dialang village. Consequently, not only patients but officiants must now walk some distance to perform the ritual.

There are no set rules that establish which of the shrines a person should visit when caught by Odieng. The members of a lineage, in one village or another, may make a habit of visiting one shrine rather than the other, but any individual may make his own choice and may change from one shrine to the other on different occasions. But after the initiation, when the youth are obligated to make confession to Odieng, all visit the shrine at Sisa's. In general, on more everyday occasions, most Ehing seem to visit Nyame rather than Karaguba.

All of the rituals I witnessed took place at Sisa's shrine. Although the elders of Karaguba allowed me to visit their shrine, they never permitted me to observe any rituals there. Though I explained, and actually rather strongly argued, that I had already seen the same ritual at Nyame, my arguments made no impression: "*munyo*" was "*munyo*." This claim, I later discovered, was directed not only toward me as a stranger to Ehing culture but also to other elders in Ehing society. No one except the participants ever attended rituals at Karaguba.

In some way, the response of the elders of Karaguba was characteristic. Older men and women are often guarded about ritual knowledge. They are thought to know things that others do not and to guard this knowledge with quick resort to the notion of *munyo,* things taboo or forbidden. Still, I do not think that the desire to keep things secret was the sole reason for Kabe's behavior at their shrine. My own impression is that their secretiveness and recalcitrance reflected what Ehing call *odzimo,* a kind of jealousy. The shrine held by Kabe, though identical in principle, had something of a secondary status in relation to Ta's shrine, perhaps because the elders of Ta's shrine not only administer to Odieng for confession but are also responsible for the grand Odieng shrine reserved for the initiation.

Amanya

Sisa Sagna today holds the title of *amanya.* This title of respect refers to the incumbent of the highest ritual role in the society. Sisa holds this title because, as the senior male in lineage Ta, he is responsible for the shrine dedicated to the initiation. And he plays the role required by the title. Wherever he goes, even just to walk about the village visiting, he carries a small broom, about a foot long and made of palm fibers. For Sisa the broom provides a sign of his office, even though he uses it as a fly swatter rather than for ritual purposes. Though I am aware that brooms are often used as ritual insignia in Africa, I rather suspect that in this case the broom is Sisa's own idea rather than a prescribed part of an *amanya*'s costume.

Then there is the costume he wears for the initiation, when he dons the colors of his office: red hat, red coat, and, for a final touch, red umbrella. I am told that this is the outfit he wore when, representative of

Fig. 2.2. Sisa Sagna, holding his broom and staff, looks on as elders perform Kamis, the hair-cutting ceremony for children.

the Ehing, he greeted Leopold L. Senghor, former President of the Republic, on a tour of the Casamance in the mid-sixties.

From the start, Sisa was gracious about my presence at his house and about my inquiry into his traditions. It was only because of his openness and generosity that I was able to observe the rituals of Odieng. In truth, had an elder other than Sisa been responsible for the rites, I might have learned much less about the spirit he serves.[7]

Rules and Social Order

In this chapter I have described the ways in which Ehing encounter Odieng in their experience—in terms of its affliction and of its ritual. There are a number of other points to be made about these encounters.

The ritual that I have described is a private rather than public affair. When the spirit attacks, victims tend to be reserved and cautious about their misfortune. The illness and circumstances are something between the spirit and the afflicted, although sometimes close kin become involved. The sick, or their kin, make their own arrangements with the elders responsible for the shrines and simply arrive at the appointed hour. I learned of most rituals only by chance, for, living next to the path that

157, 011

led from Bakunum to Nyame, I occasionally saw one or two persons walking by with the chicken and wine necessary to visit the shrine. Then I would quickly follow, on the pretense of visiting my friend Sisa. In view of these unannounced rites, the encounters I witnessed with Odieng were necessarily few in number. And past encounters were difficult to investigate. The people were loath to discuss past afflictions out of fear that even a review of the circumstances of an illness might provoke the spirit to reappear.

Apart from the feature of their privacy, I would also note that the focus of concern voiced in these rituals is not immediately connected with problems in group life. Here Odieng and its rituals contrast with much of what has been described in other work on African spirits. Take, for example, Victor Turner's studies of the intricate connection between ritual and social dynamics among the Ndembu. Ndembu spirits are often implicated in the give and take of daily life. Many times people are caught when they break kinds of social norms associated with group solidarity, authority, or the proper relations between kin and neighbors. Moreover, mystical powers may in fact be manipulated to serve political ends. The events leading to affliction are interpreted in a field of political values, and, because the spirits operate in this field, the attribution of illness and the rituals that cure are public affairs in which the individual's illness and cure mirror processes in the body politic.

As Turner (1968: 46) puts it:

> Death, disease, and misfortune are usually ascribed to tensions in local kin groups [tensions, I might add here, that often grow out of the contradictory principles of matrilineal descent and virilocal residence that organize Ndembu society], expressed as personal grudges charged with the mystical power of sorcery or witchcraft, or as beliefs in the punitive action of ancestor spirits. Diviners try to elicit from their clients responses which give them clues to the current tensions in their groups of origin. Divination becomes a form of social analysis.

One might also add here, as Turner has documented, that the illness of the victim may, in some cases, be interpreted as a projection of guilt or anxiety. I am not doing my duty toward my lineage kin, and I become sick: the ancestor spirit is an externalization of my ambivalence.

To understand Odieng, it is important to observe just how different Odieng and its rules are from this kind of spiritual activity. Though other Ehing spirits—like Echin which attacks the children of parents who are arguing about rice—do, as in Ndembu concepts, work to externalize social tension, Odieng's affliction seems to stand apart from everyday life. I have no evidence that diagnoses of Odieng are made more frequently when social relations are difficult. I would also point out that the rules themselves do not refer to conventions that directly regulate group amity or individual obligations. Seeing cadavers or mixing wine and water has nothing directly to do with the myriad tensions that habitually arise in Ehing social relations. And the ritual at Odieng's shrine has nothing in common with the group experiences that accompany Ndembu treatment of affliction. There is no sharing of a problem by a local community, no airing of grievances to reduce social tensions. There is no cure of the social body along with the cure of the physical. With Odieng, hardly anyone need know of an affliction, hardly anyone need see its cure. The rules of Odieng, in short, have little to do with political integration or political power.

What counts with Odieng, I want to claim, are the rules themselves, as a structure of ideas. The task, then, in interpreting Odieng is to explore the meaning of these rules as a conceptual system and to see in this meaning the source of the spirit's power.

PART II

~~~

The House

"Relinquish," McCaslin said. "Relinquish. You, the direct male descendants of him who saw the opportunity and took it, bought the land, took the land, got the land no matter how, held it to bequeath, no matter how, out of the old grant, the first patent, when it was a wilderness of wild beasts of wilder men, and cleared it, translated it into something to bequeathe to his children, worthy of bequeathing for his descendants' ease and security and pride and to perpetuate his name and accomplishments."
—William Faulkner, *Go Down, Moses*

3

The Locality of Men

The point to begin an interpretation of Odieng is with its central separation—the separation of the sexes. Ehing are explicit that the rules about initiation and birth are the most serious part of the spirit's work. As they put it, Odieng has drawn a cloth between men and women, and each sex must stay on its own side.

If one were to ask why the spirit has set up this division, the people have little to say. They simply restate that the sexes must stay apart because it is a *munyo* (taboo) of Odieng. But they will develop their own view of sexual classification by telling a story that characterizes the relations between men and women. Within a short time during my stay in the field, I was given an abbreviated version of the story. Later on, I found a man who offered a more complete tale, and it is this text I relate here. It is the story of the origin of marriage, and a tale that, in its cryptic way, contains the core ideas of Ehing sexuality that are the point of Odieng's rules.

A Marriage Tale

When God sent man and woman to earth, the woman dug a hole in which she sat. The man said that he'd join her there, but she refused. So her

31

husband said, he said, "Hah, didn't he say for us to sit in there?" But the woman said, "No, I don't want that," and she hit the man. At that time the man didn't have force in his hands, nothing. Yes, he didn't have hands.

After a time, God descended to visit them. He found the man quite beaten. The man said, "She killed me. You said that she is good but, when I went to stay with her, she refused and hit me. Where will I stay?" God called the woman and told her to sit with the man. The woman said, "How so! He is no good. He wants to see what I do." God told her to come. When she arrived, he seized her hands and pulled! pulled out! pulled out! She didn't have any more force.

God told the man to come and said, "I'll show you the house. You will build a house." God told the man to draw water, and he went to build. The man built and built. The man went for wood and constructed the ceiling. God said, "Hurry, the rain is about to fall. When it falls the woman will come stay with you here." "She who tried to kill me? Never!" God said, "Oh, no? Wait."

The man went to the fields and he brought back straw. He cut the straw and bound it; then God told him to attach it to the house. God said, "Cover! The rain is coming!"

For three days it rained. It rained! It rained! It rained! The water entered the hole of the woman. The woman ran out of the hole saying, "Waaa! Where will I stay now?" She went to find the man and said, "I want to stay here." But the man refused. "No. You chased me from your hole; now our father showed me this house and told me to sit here." The woman retorted, "Ha! as I am stronger than you, we'll go fight today." They fought, and the man hit her and chased her away.

The woman went and said to God, "The rain came and ruined my house. It's no good." God said, "But isn't the other person there?" The woman responded, "He is there. But when I said that we'll stay together, he refused. We fought and he hit me until my body became hot." God told her, "Return; tell him that I said he should live with you, that I sent you from the sky to the earth so that you will have a person like I had you."

She went and told that to the man, but he refused. She returned to God who told her to try again, but the man still refused. When she returned again, God told her to sit down. She sat down. God said, "Take this string of beads and attach it around your hips." She attached the string. God said, "Look there again, which beads are prettier?" She selected more beads, and attached those also.

God said, "Now go to him again. When he wants to refuse, cross near to him and resonate the beads with your hands. They will sound YEES. When the beads make this, you will stay." She went and, when the man sent her away, she resonated the string of beads. It sounded YEES. He said,

"Come back, come back." She said, "But you told me to leave." He said, "No, no, come back."

She returned. When she returned, they lay down together. Marriage came from there.

Implications of the Text

The problem in the story is how the sexes are to be united, and it is an issue presented and worked out through the possibilities and alternatives of residence. In the beginning of the text, the woman lives in a hole and the man lacks any sort of habitation. The initial scene, then, is one of potential matrilocal residence. But the story shows that a man without shelter is a man without "force"; for, when he approaches the woman to sit in her hole, he is physically beaten off. The woman is the stronger, as even a hole in the ground is better than no place to live at all.

The possession of shelter may be symbolic of something more than strength, for the word I have translated as "force" (*semben*) may also be used to refer to sexual potency. The language and action of the tale, therefore, may be alluding to the man's lack of virility, an allusion given some substance by the curious detail that he is without "hands." It is because of a lack of strength or of virility (and these may never be completely dissociated in Ehing thought) that the man cannot force his way into the woman's hole. In sharp contrast, as we shall see, to actual practice, he is faced with the problem of where to stay.

The story at this point also offers another reason why the woman herself actively rejects the man: "He wants to see what I do." Although an indefinite expression, its meaning is fairly obvious to anyone familiar with the culture. What women most emphatically do is give birth, and that sight is prohibited to men. The woman in the tale rightly insists that the "cover" between the sexes be maintained. The text, then, can be seen as focusing on the dilemma that reproduction involves both the union and the separation of the sexes, and this tension is conveyed through a dialectic of residence. It is a tension that pervades the social relations between men and women not only in the tale but in real life as well.

That reproduction is the crux of the matter becomes clearer when God intervenes and endeavors to mediate the couple's separation, for he sent them from the sky "to have a child." God's first step is to rectify the man's lack of housing. And building becomes an activity through which the man gains hands, or the force to use them. At the same time, his gain is emphasized by the woman's loss: the reversal in relative strength perfectly mirrors the reversal in relative shelters. But the building of a house only sets up the possibility of cohabitation; it does not ensure either its certitude or inevitability. The man and woman are now left with separate residences, one above ground and the other below.

To move the woman, God makes the woman's shelter inadequate by sending rain. Rain is God's instrument, and it should be recalled here that God and rain are denoted by a single term. Rain in the story pushes the sexes together, as in everyday life it brings them into the joint labor of producing rice.

Even with the rain, however, a solution is not readily found. It is now the man who rejects the woman, as he refuses to forgive their past conflict. Inferentially, we also surmise that she is not attractive to him, and this brings about a structural symmetry in the story as it balances the man's previous physical deficiency. And so God gives her beads, as he gave the man a house (and "hands"), and their sibilance against her hips breaks down the man's reluctance.

The motif of beads is suggestive of the underlying source of the woman's undesirability. In everyday life women may wear beads around their hips at any time except when they are menstruating and when they have recently given birth. Hence, when women are not wearing beads, they are associated with blood, and contact with them is a taboo of Odieng. Apparently, in the past young women were known to have manipulated this signal of unavailability as a defense against rape; when pursued, they would discreetly throw off their beads and, by that action, simulate a state of interdiction. In view of these customs, one reading of the story is that the woman without beads is implicitly associated with blood and reproduction, and this association makes her both undesirable and unavailable. An allusion to female blood and birth has, in fact, been made earlier in the story when the woman demands her privacy. When she wears the beads, the woman is removed from any state in which she would be dangerous to the man; she therefore becomes desirable.

The story ends on a note of apparent resolution: men and women are to lie down together. And yet, this resolution would seem to leave a major question completely unsettled. If a man cannot see what a woman does, why should a difference of place matter? Why his place and not hers? Nothing in the story bears on this puzzle. Instead, what is made unequivocal is simply that one mode of residence works and the other does not. That is the moral of the tale.

The Building

Malinowski once argued that the purpose of myth was to establish a charter for basic social institutions and practices (Malinowski 1954: 10). In this case, his view would prove accurate, in the sense that the text does correspond to Ehing practice: women do move into the houses that men build. But this tale is much more than a charter. Building houses, the movement of women, and the connection of these events to reproduction are all fundamental elements of Ehing social theory. To discover the meanings of these elements is to explore the ideas about gender that are integral to Odieng's separations.

In this chapter I begin to explore what gives the concept of a house so much force and why it is so central to Ehing notions of sexual relations. The answer rests in a double meaning of the word *edop,* "house." The term is used to refer both to the sturdy dwellings in which individual families live and to groups of persons who are related through descent. Since the tale focuses on the building itself, I take the physical sense of house as my point of departure.

Ehing are proud of their houses, especially their permanancy. Most houses remain standing for a good fifteen years, and I have visited some over fifty years old. In its basic design, a house is a thicked-walled cube formed from dried mud and capped with a thatched roof. It measures some 12 meters to a side. A hall transects the middle of the house and doubles as a public room, where a family often eats, and as a passageway into the rear courtyard. There are two rooms to each side of the hall, each with its own small door. Each adult member of a family has a separate bedroom; small children sleep with a parent of the same sex—on mats made from palm leaves—and adolescents may claim a room of their own. Granaries are built into the bedrooms as a platform that extends over much of the room, on top of which sit baskets of rice bundles.

The combination of arching thatch roof and mud ceiling relieves the heat of the dry season. The air inside a house is noticeably crisper than outside, and the walls are cool to the touch. A few individuals, however, have invested in corrugated tin roofing, which is quite expensive in comparison with straw. The metallic roof, however, does not have to be repaired every few years, as does thatch. But tin retains heat and, during parts of the year, can make a house exceedingly uncomfortable.

A house conveys a sense of privacy. There are front and back doors, which are tied shut or locked whenever the family is away or at a village gathering. They are also shut tight at night. There is at most one window per room, and each is small, some with wooden slats. In part, the lack of windows may be attributed to a defense against mosquitoes; before the Ehing could purchase netting, many would light fires in their rooms at night so that the smoke would drive out the insects. In part, also, the enclosed sense of space in a house—and the rooms are quite dark, even in bright daylight—may be associated with security against witchcraft.

Outside the house, a fence of palm fronds circles away from each side

granary

Fig. 3.1. Ehing house (with cutaway).

wall and around the rear to form a back courtyard. It is here that a family spends most of its time—weaving baskets, carving belts for climbing the palms, spending evenings with friends. The yard is scattered with the stools that comprise the major furniture belonging to a family.

Building takes place during the dry season and may take two months to complete. The walls are built up out of wet, compressed mud in a series of stages. Each section of wall, set about 60 centimeters high and 20 centimeters thick, is set and allowed to dry several days before the next layer is added. Once the walls and ceiling are finished, the builders often wait several weeks before attending to the roof. Wood supports must be cut, collected, and transported; adequate thatch must be located and dressed. I have seen some individuals put off these final tasks so long that the first rains had already arrived before the house was fully covered. God's warning to hurry in the marriage tale often proves to be good advice.

For the first layer of wall, a man can count on the help of his village mates; and a wife can count on the help of her friends to cut and carry the thatch to the site. For the rest, a man works with one or two friends or relatives, help he will repay in time.

Perhaps the most important statement to be made about houses is that, as the myth tells us, they are built only by men. It is because men build houses, Ehing say today as they said in the myth, that men are sedentary and that women move in marriage. The meaning of this contrast is fundamental, but to understand it we have to explore the other sense of the word *edop,* the concept of house as a category of descent.

The House as Descent Group

According to Ehing tradition, Houses as lineages owe their origin to the time when people came from the south, looking for land suitable to convert into rice fields. In the context of this tradition, building a physical house and founding a House as a lineage were contemporaneous events. The descent groups found today in Ehing society are thought to be named after these first builders and first claimants to land. In Bakunum village, for example, the members of House Buzenu (Edop Buzenu) are the descendants in a male line from Abuzenu, and those of House Kula from the man named Akula.

Though the people believe that the founders of Houses lived in a vague and distant past, this passage of time is not reflected in any ordered genealogical line. Most Ehing remember the names of their relatives only to the generation of grandfather and, when pressed to continue, either claim no further knowledge or jump to the name of the founder of their House. The members of a House who do not share a grandfather cannot trace precisely how they are related. At most, the elders of a House will state that their "fathers" were "brothers." A few elders did know the names of great-grandfathers, but no effort was made to order the relations of House members by means of a genealogical calculus characteristic of segmentary systems.[1]

Houses typically are groups of not more than thirty adult men and women. The male members of a House are expected to live together, in a rough circle of houses around a central courtyard. The building of the houses themselves is coordinated with the marriages of each son in a family. When an individual receives a bride, he at first lives with her in his father's house, often for two or three years. During this time, the couple eat rice that comes from the father's fields and save the crop that they gain from their own. Then, at the start of the dry season of the third year, the son starts construction and moves in by the rains. With a separate dwelling, the couple begin to rely on their own food resources. The pattern is the same for each son but the last, who often remains in, and eventually inherits, his father's house.

A house, then, is the site of various social arrangements. A younger man lives with his wives and children; an elder, at periods in his life, is

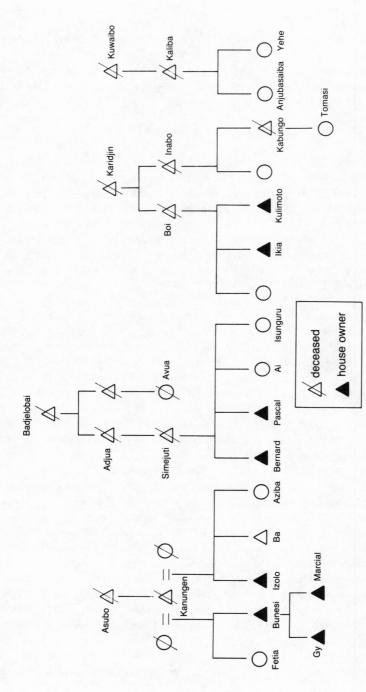

Fig. 3.2. Genealogy of Bazolo House.

host to his sons and their wives, and sometimes to their small children. In point of fact, however, the actual circumstances of residence often are still more varied. Many households in the villages provide shelter for a score of persons at a time. For example, at the dissolution of their marriages, a common occurrence, women return to live with their fathers or brothers, often for long periods. Or, when a husband dies, a woman may elect either to return to a brother or to move in with one of her adult sons. And still again, Ehing engage in various, temporary forms of fostering: sick children are often sent to live with their maternal relatives. All these circumstances lead to a more fluid living situation than a description of the developmental cycle of households might at first suggest.

Edop Bazolo, in Bakunum, depicted in Figure 3.2, provides a good example of a House's genealogy and of the basic way that the notion of a House organizes residence. All of the adult male members are coresident, except for an individual named Ba. Authority in the group is exercised by Bunesi and Kulimoto, who administer any shrines found on Bazolo's land. In 1977, when I collected this information, the elder women of the House were living at the houses where they married, though some of the younger women were at Ziguinchor during the dry season. Ba had, at that time, already abandoned his house for some years. He had become sick after his divorce, and he went to recover and stay with his maternal kin in another House in the village. He sleeps there but cooks and eats his own rice separately.

The Kahin Spirit

The concept of descent, Sally Falk Moore has suggested, is a notion about identity. It is "a way of thinking about the procession of the generations . . . that postulates certain identities between ancestors and descendants and consequently also categorizes contemporaries" (1969: 381). For Ehing, this notion of identity is inextricably bound up with a spirit named Kahin. In terms of an understanding of Odieng and the problem of separations, this spirit is the single most important concept to understand about Houses as descent groups.

Every lineage possesses its own Kahin spirit and shrine. The spirit is represented by a forked stick made from a hard wood. These shrines are usually found in the ground against the outside wall of a standing house and are often encircled by a mud wall about 10 centimeters high. Kahin are also found at the sites where houses once stood and, when not in use, are hardly noticeable under the cover of high grass and weeds. The shrines of Kahin may be moved when necessary.

Ehing hold that each original immigrant planted the shrine of a Kahin in the ground when he built his house and claimed land: the shrine was installed to mark what was to become the identity of his descendants, and to mark the land that he claimed for them. Kahin, then, are used to define the origin of lineages, and, when Ehing express their membership in the same House, they say, "We have the same Kahin."

Some sense of how Ehing still conceive of this tradition may be illustrated by the Kahin associated with the building of my own house. When the first layer of wall had been laid out to dry in the sun, Mossi Bassene, my sponsor in Bakunum, suggested that a Kahin be installed. I agreed, and arranged for 10 liters of palm wine, one liter for the ceremony of installation and the rest for the village elders who would come to witness the event. On the proper day Mossi arrived with my wine, and a small stick shaped like a Y. Two elders planted the stick in the sand in the middle of the house; then, in characteristic fashion when praying to a spirit, they spoke while dripping wine from a libation pitcher after each phrase. The elders asked the spirit that we (that is, my wife and myself) find *mazunemi*—a word connoting peace and well-being—while at Bakunum and that we should soon find children as well. Then the elders asked that our car, a Citroën 2-CV, remain in good repair, a practical point that, I soon enough learned, clearly fell on deaf ears. Once our house was complete, the Kahin was moved, without ceremony, to just outside a side wall.

In its contemporary role, the work of the Kahin spirit is bound up with central ideas concerning rice, land, fertility, and transition. The Kahin is the site of many rites of passage at birth, marriage, and death. Also, youth gather to libate and ask for well-being at the Kahin before they enter the initiation forest, and lineages celebrate the harvest at the same shrine. Unlike other spirits they know, Ehing do not usually address Kahin when someone is caught, for this spirit is not directly associated with affliction. Only when rituals at the Kahin have been neglected might Ehing think of the spirit as the cause of some misfortune. I have seen, for example, the infertility of young women attributed to the discovery that their parents neglected to perform Kamis (a cutting of hair at the Kahin) for them when they were infants.

When elders go to the Kahin to perform rituals—to pray and offer gifts of wine—they characteristically begin the libation by calling out the names of ancestors. Very often, though not invariably, they begin with the House founder and then add the names of three or four elders who are believed to have once officiated at the shrines. These names are not evoked in any consistent order, and on different occasions different names might be mentioned. Names of persons thought long dead might be called out, as well as the name of a father or grandfather. In no instance did Ehing believe they were invoking names that represent the passage of time in a line from the past to the present. Instead of trying to represent through the names a line of descent, the elders are more directly linking themselves to the spirit, the Kahin of their House.

Houses and Land

I have said that the people associate the placing of Kahin with the original claiming and clearing of their land. The shrines located today by their houses are a record of the division of their territory into separate estates. And therefore, just as the Kahin is a vehicle that defines group membership, it is a vehicle that defines the connection of Houses to land. In the Ehing idiom, "Kahin and land are one."

With this statement, Ehing mean that all rights to land are based on original claims. The founders of Houses staked out both rice fields and upland, and these claims serve as a charter for the present holdings of their descendants. In Ehing social theory, the fields an individual man or woman farms are part of the legacy based on these original claims—they are the fields that have been passed down, within the House, for generations.

It is in light of this history that Ehing account for the size and location of a House's land. When Ehing say the "Kahin and land are one," they do not imply that the paddy plots of a House are all contiguous. Founders are thought to have claimed land in various villages—though the largest holdings lie close to the upland where the ancestor planted his Kahin. The point is that members of a House hold rights to paddy fields that are widely scattered. The amount of land of a House is also said to reflect initial events. A case in point is House Bazolo which has much upland but relatively little paddy. I was told by the elders of Bazolo that their ancestor was busy making a rope to tie up his cattle when others were out staking their claims. As he was late in reaching the plains, his children today are always out asking to borrow fields.

This ancestral charter and especially the idea that the "Kahin and land are one" are what link the physical location of men—the building of their houses so stressed in the marriage text—to the concept of descent. As men do the building of houses, they are sedentary, and they build on land belonging to the group. Ideally, the male members of a House build at the Kahin and close to their rice fields. They live together around a single courtyard (*omiro*).

This is the normative pattern of Ehing social organization, and it is a

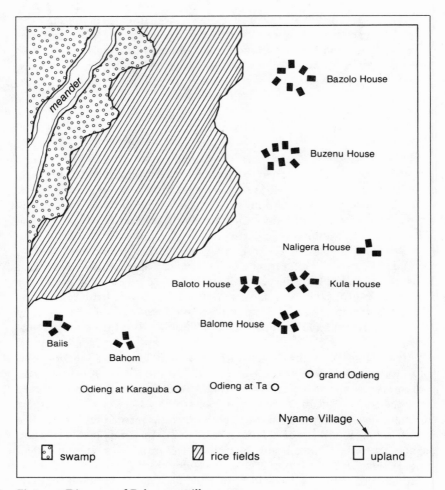

Bazolo House

Buzenu House

Naligera House

Baloto House

Kula House

Balome House

Baiis

Bahom

grand Odieng

Odieng at Karaguba

Odieng at Ta

Nyame Village

▣ swamp   ▨ rice fields   ▢ upland

Fig. 3.3. Diagram of Bakunum village.

pattern that often is realized in actual social arrangements. But, as I have already noted, some individuals do spend some time living in other households. And more significantly, some men may not only move temporarily but may actually decide to build away from the houses of their lineal group. In these circumstances, a man may go off and live in isolation in the woods, or he may decide to build near someone who already has moved off his House's land. In either case, since all the land of the village belongs to some House, anyone who builds away from his own land must ask permission from the House on whose land he intends to live.

Ehing distinguish between the clusters of houses occupied by members of the same House and the clusters composed of people who are not related. In daily speech, people refer to the latter groups by using the name of the tract of bush or forest where they are located. In the case of Bakunum village, two such groups are called Baiis and Bahom (see Fig. 3.3).

The circumstances that led to the formation of these groups almost always involved problems of illness or fears of witchcraft. These problems and fears are attributed to tension brought about by living with one's kin or to tension between women who have married into the House. In the Ehing idiom, these tensions arise because of the *odzimo*, "jealousy," of others. The story of Alfred, which I had a chance to observe directly, provides a good illustration of the complicated circumstances that precede a change of residence.

Alfred originally constructed his house next to that of his father, Bunwar, who lived there with his second wife, not the mother of Alfred. Alfred's mother had left when Bunwar remarried. One year when Alfred was away to find work during the dry season, his wife found it difficult to sleep. Her body was "heavy" and "tired," and I was told that she dreamed of a witch. At the time she made no accusation but simply alerted Alfred to return to the village. He did so, and telling his kin that his wife was sick, he took her for several months to Ziguinchor, the regional capital. They returned to the village several months later, when Alfred heard through village gossip (specifically, from his father's sisters) that Bunwar's wife had been telling everyone who would listen that Alfred had led his wife away because he thought she was a witch. Alfred denied ever having made such an accusation.

Bunwar's wife was quite unhappy at their return. She refused to greet Alfred's wife, which, in an Ehing village, is a serious breach of etiquette. She also refused any gifts from Alfred's wife, though she accepted small fish and other items from Alfred himself. At this time, Alfred's one-year-old infant became quite ill. The child suffered from coughing and from swollen limbs and stomach. Alfred proposed the family go to the spirit Echin, for these were the spirit's symptoms when there was tension within the family. At the shrine, the officiant told Bunwar's wife that no one had accused her of being a witch and that she had no right to be so abusive. After the ceremony, the child became well.

But Bunwar's wife was still angry, and two years later conflict again surfaced. Apparently the chickens of Bunwar's wife habitually strayed around Alfred's house, but his stepmother did not want the fowl to sleep there. Therefore at night, she would reach in the closed door to sweep up the chickens without greeting Alfred's wife. At this time a curer from a neighboring Diola group visited to look into the health of Alfred's two children. As is the custom, Alfred killed a chicken to provide the visitor with an appropriate meal. Several days later, Bunwar's wife reported that she had lost a chicken, and she accused Alfred's wife of taking it to feed their visitor. To carry her accusation, Bunwar's wife gave Alfred some eggs, meaning that "since you've already stolen the bird, you might as well have the eggs." Alfred's wife refused to accept the eggs; Alfred took them back and exchanged angry words with his stepmother.

At this point the second of Alfred's children became sick. The elders of the House decided that all must go back to the spirit Echin. But Bunwar's wife refused to go. To coax her, the elders told her that she was not a witch but that to refuse to go to save the child would be an action tantamount to witchcraft. There was a large meeting at which Bunwar took the side of his wife against Alfred and his wife. Finally Bunwar's wife shouted out, "What I want, what I decided, is that the child should die. Because Alfred's wife called me a witch, now I'll prove it." In the face of her intransigence, the meeting broke up.

The child died shortly afterwards. During the next dry season, Alfred built a new house, still in Bakunum, but deep in the woods belonging to another lineage.

There are a number of points I want to stress about this case. Though this situation was a very difficult one and should not be thought of as characteristic, it does give a sense of the kind of chronic tensions that arise from living in close quarters. It also illustrates the kind of solution Ehing seek in order to avoid witches: they try to distance themselves from whoever might be jealous—they move away. Bunwar's wife, in all minds, was an extraordinarily difficult woman. By all accounts, as a woman who herself had not had children, she was motivated by jealousy, the emotion thought to direct the desire to harm others. To escape the danger and tension, Alfred built far off in the woods, though still in the proximity of one other neighbor, named Kushie.

Kushie's case involves a more complex history. His grandfather originally lived in Dialang, but he was sick and decided to move to Kalian. He died there at a young age. His wife then took her son, Kushie's father, back to her kin at Bakunum, where Kushie was raised. And so, when he came of age, he decided to continue to live there rather than to return to build with the other members of his House.

The ties between members of these local groups of unrelated people (like Alfred and Kushie) are limited to cooperation in everyday projects, such as digging a well, and sporadic help in other forms of work. I should note that, although Alfred sought to protect his family by escaping the jealousy of his stepmother, he did not move very far. His new house was only a 15-minute walk from his father's. Alfred could not, in actuality, move very far from his rice fields and from the Kahin where he often had need to perform and to participate in rituals. Ehing note that those who have sought the protection of isolation often eventually move back to the lineage's courtyard.

Harvest

In jural terms, the notion that the "Kahin and land are one" is expressed in a system of rights by which the members of a House gain land to work their fields and to build their houses.[2] But it is in ritual and symbolic terms that Ehing express for themselves their conception of the link between House and land. Although Ehing lineages are rightly described as land-holding corporations, this statement is not a fully adequate representation of the social facts or how they must be understood.

A ritual that reveals the Ehing conception of a House and its connection to land is the one that celebrates the first fruits, the new harvest of rice. The ritual is called Ihin, and significantly the name of the rite is derived from the same root as the word for the Kahin spirit.

In the morning on the day of Ihin, two elders of each House visit their Kahin to offer a gift of wine. As they libate, the elders ask for the well-being (mazunemi) of the members of the House, of their domestic animals, and of the rice which is about to be harvested. They add also the plea that "all those who have come here today go home with a child"—that is, that all the wives married into the House become pregnant. Meanwhile, the wives of the House members have begun to cook rice for an afternoon meal. They cook together in large iron pots, pots which hold a bundle's worth of new rice brought by each man of the lineage. The elders take a bowlful of rice from this pot when they visit the Kahin again several hours after their first libation. The rice is carried in a wooden bowl and covered with cow's milk; and the elders are accompanied on this visit by all the younger children of the lineage. For the ritual, one elder tosses a spoonful of rice to each side of the Kahin and carefully places a third at the spirit's base. He then sets the bowl down on the ground, and, at his signal, the children leap forward, each to grab and swallow a handful of the new crop. Then all return to the house of an elder to join their parents in the thanksgiving meal.

In this ritual Ehing communicate, in a symbolic language that is quite straightforward, the unity of House, land, and Kahin. The members of the House, who have worked their own individual fields, pool their rice in a commensal meal. The children of the House are fed the first of the new rice at the shrine that marks the inception of their group, and rice and children are paired as the group's major accomplishments.

Still, during Ihin, there is another and more dramatic expression of the equation that "the Kahin and land are one." This expression involves situations when a House has become "extinguished" (when all its members have already died) or when only women remain.

Ehing are keenly aware of the possibility of rapid population changes in the size of a House. In the environment of the Casamance, illness may cause a precipitous fall in the membership of a group; in 1977 there were several Houses with only two or three adults left. It is understandable, then, that in their prayers elders often ask that Houses prosper and grow, and I would note that some Houses that had faced difficult times not long ago are once again "full." But I also learned the names of various Houses that were less fortunate and are "extinguished." In this situation, the Kahin remains and is inherited by another, delegated House.

The relationship of inheriting responsibility for Kahin and rights to the land defined by the spirit is known as *butaino,* a word that one informant traced to the verb "to inherit." *Butaino* are always members of Houses who share a patronym. Sometimes these inheritors owe their origin to a single House that at one time segmented, but other *butaino* had no other connection to each other than the *butaino* relationship itself.

Now at Ihin, the actions of *butaino* spell out the link between Kahin and land. A House that has inherited the land of another libates and cooks rice not only at their own shrine but also at the shrine of the extinguished lineage. The rice they place at the shrine has been harvested from the inherited land. There are, of course, no children to grab the rice, but the Kahin endures as the spirit which defines an area of land in perpetuity.

4

The Movement of Women

In the last chapter, I began to explain the implications of the marriage tale by focusing on the concept of "house." We have seen that, in Ehing social thought, a man without a house is a man "without force." And we have traced this image to the double meaning of the word *edop*—to the fact that a house refers not only to a building but to a category of descent. It is this doubleness of meaning that gives the image of the house so much weight. Building becomes an image of the power to create a line of descent. Still, the analysis of the text so far leaves much unresolved. It is still unclear in any precise sense just why, in Ehing thought, building a house conveys this sense of descent. And it is unclear as well just why, as the text dictates, a woman must move in marriage. In this chapter, I take up these issues.

   The key to these questions is found in a conception Ehing hold about reproduction. God, after all, sent man and woman to earth to have a child, and it is this goal which precipitated the tension in the text. The conception that is so crucial is that human beings possess, and are given life by, souls and that the source of these souls is "the rice fields."

A Cycle of Souls

The notion of souls in Ehing thought is characterized by a cycle of reincarnation. The people articulate a complex doctrine in which the soul is divided into three conceptual phases, identified by separate indigenous terms, which take the soul from the land into a person and then into the land until reborn.

The phase of the soul that animates a person's body (*enyi*) and gives it life is known as *da*. *Da,* in turn, is divided into two "sides"; the left *da* and the right *da*. Often when a person is ill, it is because a witch has stolen his left *da* and hidden it; once the left *da* is found (I have been told it looks like a spider) and returned, the person is cured. But a person cannot live without his right *da*. This is the true, invisible soul, the soul that sees in dreams, and when this *da* has left the body, the person has lost his life.

The soul *da* transforms at the end of a life into the phase of the soul called *afuga*. The word used for this transformation is literally "to fall" (*kalolo*); the *da* is said "to fall" *afuga* (*kalolo afuga*). *Afuga* is the soul that has left the body to live "in the rice fields." No elaboration is given of this underworld; the people simply say that a soul lives there with other souls (*kufuga,* plural of *afuga*) of his lineage.

The "fall" of *da* into *afuga* sometimes does not seem to correspond strictly to corporeal life and death. Sometimes, as a person approaches death, his true *da* may leave the body before it is fully inanimate. For example, if a dying person begins to call out the names of his ancestors, witnesses may say "his *da* is already gone."

The second phase of the soul (*afuga*) lives in the ground until it, in turn, "falls" into the soul called *agun*. *Agun* is the soul that has left the rice fields and fallen into a woman's body in order to be born. It is the soul that roughly corresponds to our notion of fetus, but, again, this correspondence is not always exact. The *agun* may remain even after the child is born before passing into the phase called *da,* the phase at which I began. I was told that the soul of an infant may not be *da* until he recognizes through his smile and behavior the differences between kin and strangers.

In theory, a soul is reborn every fourth generation and returns to enter a body of the same sex as its previous incarnation. In conjunction with this doctrine of returning souls, Ehing sometimes give children the names of their great-grandparents.

When I describe here the cycle of souls, I refer to a religious belief and not an everyday assumption, for Ehing do not habitually think of persons as returned souls. In fact, when I pressed them for evidence, they cited only a few general cases as examples. One case concerns any child who is born with a deformity, especially of the ear or finger. My informants gave the following explanation: The soul in question was thought responsible for a series of infant deaths: it had repeatedly left the body of infants it had entered. To stop this behavior, and my informants are here referring to past events, elders were thought to have cut the child on the lobe or finger, to mark it. In Ehing thought, a soul once recognized for its destructive behavior would cease to cause so much suffering. And so, when a child in contemporary times is born with a deformity, it stands as evidence of its own past history. Once the body has been cut, the mark shows on all future bodies this soul will inhabit.

Interestingly enough, a similar set of beliefs is found among the Igbo of Nigeria. A graphic description is offered by Chinua Achebe in his novel *Things Fall Apart*. After the death of a woman's second child—and she was to lose nine in all—the diagnosis was made that the infant was "one of those wicked children who, when they died, entered their mothers' wombs to be born again." When the third child then died, and significantly on the same day it had been born, the marking of the child was ordered. Achebe (1958: 55) writes:

> The medicine man then ordered that there should be no mourning. He brought a sharp razor from the goatskin bag slung from his left shoulder and began to mutilate the child. . . . After such treatment it would think twice before coming again, unless it was one of the stubborn ones who returned, carrying the stamp of their mutilation—a missing finger or perhaps a dark line where the medicineman's razor had cut them.

Although the Ehing have a more optimistic view of the procedure and its results, the ideas are very close.

The other form of evidence used by Ehing to point out the cycle of souls concerns borrowed and disputed property. There is the story, for example, of a man who borrowed from another a log from a fan palm to use in the construction of his house. Years later, after the borrower had died, the owner of the log came to the descendants of the deceased and asked, not for the log, but for a bar of iron which he claimed had been the object taken. "Since your 'father' is dead, you didn't know, but give it back now." As the owner was about to hand over the valuable iron, a child in the house intervened and showed his father the log still in the house; he said that this was in reality the object borrowed, for he was the one who had asked for it originally.

Marriage Ritual

It is in the light of these notions of the soul that one must interpret the social logic of the marriage tale and the contrast it presents between the sedentariness of men and the movement of women. To demonstrate, I will describe the rituals that communicate the voyage of the soul. First, I describe the marriage ritual that calls the soul from the land; then, the mortuary ritual in which the soul is sent back to the rice fields.

The language used by the Ehing to refer to marriage corresponds exactly to the final outcome in the marriage myth. Women "walk" when they marry, and men "receive." The ritual that organizes a woman's walk to a man's house is called "Holding Out the Spoon" (*Kanyul Kahielo*).

"Holding Out the Spoon" was traditionally preceded by a series of gifts of wine. Because these gifts are now offered infrequently, I will offer only a brief description of them. When a man decided to marry, he inaugurated negotiations by sending a gourd of wine via an intermediary to the woman's parents. Her father would ask his daughter whether they should accept the wine. An affirmative response gave the suitor an initial claim to reproductive rights; thereafter, if the woman should decide against the marriage, her suitor in theory could block the mouth of this gourd with leaves, hang it upside down from the roof of his house, and by that action block the woman's fertility.

Immediately after the first gourd was accepted, the suitor sent a gift of about 10 liters to the woman's lineage as a group. For the next three years, he made an annual gift of wine ranging from 30 to 60 liters. Following a similar prestation in the fourth year, he and his village age-mates contributed an even larger gift of wine to the members of the woman's village. This prestation was known as "asking" and increased the groom's claim, for now, if the marriage were not realized, the suitor might demand compensation of a rice field from the woman's father. Finally, the following year the suitor presented a single gourd, called "the gourd of the person who spins cotton," to the woman's mother. The mother either drank the wine, which signaled that her daughter would begin the move to her husband's house, or refused the gourd and asked that it be brought again the next year if she considered her daughter still too young to marry.

According to tradition, a bride never moved directly to her husband's house, but first spent about a week at the house of a friend of the groom. The friend, acting as an intermediary, is called "he who encloses," for the new bride is enclosed in a room of his house. Sometimes, before the woman was led away, her father libated at his lineage shrine to ask that she marry in good health, peace, and "be pregnant by the time the rains appear."

The bride then entered a period of time called *buwun* which lasted about two weeks. During the first week at the friend's, she sat all day on a new mat in a room of the house and passed her time spinning cotton. She was not to perform any other work. She was decorated with bracelets and continuously provided with palm wine which neighborhood children came to share. I was told that she was allowed to leave the house only once in the morning and once at dusk for natural functions.

At the end of the week, the intermediary escorted the woman to her husband's house (more precisely, his father's house, where the couple first resided). She was still in *buwun* and, therefore, still did no work. For about three days she slept in a room with her husband's mother or sister. Then one night her husband entered his room to find his wife on the bed. To commemorate their union, the couple exchanged loincloths at that time, which had been given to each by their mothers. This was the first sexual contact between the couple; for, though Ehing did not necessarily marry as virgins, no contact was condoned between prospective spouses. Several days later the couple performed "Holding Out the Spoon."

Ehing say that without the performance of this rite "the couple aren't really married." In this procedure, husband, wife, and husband's sister sit on a mat placed in front of the husband's lineage shrine—the Kahin. The husband places a gourd of wine, and the sister a pot of cooked rice, at its base. A lineage elder, often the groom's father, pours wine from the gourd into a libation pitcher, and, as he speaks, he slowly drips wine on the shrine. The elder states that his son now has a wife, and he addresses the souls of the lineage, asking that whichever of them wants to "fall *agun* with the couple sitting here" should "go home" with them. The elder then pours some of the wine from the pitcher in a cow's horn, picks up sand from the base of the lineage shrine, and mixes it in with the wine. He gives some of the mixture to the bride, who takes a mouthful and spits it out to her left and right; she then is given another mouthful which she swallows. The elder gives the horn to the husband, who also spits and swallows. The husband's sister then takes the cooked rice from the shrine and offers some on a wooden spoon to the in-marrying woman, who puts a handful in her mouth, spits it out, and then takes another mouthful which she swallows. Again, the husband repeats the same actions. Witnesses then throw sand from the base of the lineage shrine and surrounding area onto the mat. The mat is rolled up with the sand still on it and taken inside the husband's house. The couple sleep on it that night.

At this point I want only to focus on the action that directly evokes the connection between land and marriage. The people explicitly associate the sand from the base of the shrine with the fields that belong to the lineage. In more precise terms, the sand is a metonym for the souls that are housed in the earth. By drinking the sand, and then having intercourse on their sandy mat, the newly married couple symbolically enact the movement of a soul coming to "rest within the woman." With "Holding Out the Spoon," the Ehing say, an *agun* knows "a woman has come."

Although the people insisted to me that "Holding Out the Spoon" invariably was performed at the beginning of marriages, it is today, along with other customs, sometimes neglected. With the extensive dry-season migrations to Ziguinchor and Dakar, much of the traditional marriage system has been abandoned. But when "Holding Out the Spoon" is not performed, Ehing contend that the lineage shrine is liable to "catch" the wife, which means that she will be unable to become pregnant. As the elders say, "If you don't give the woman a spoon, she won't have a stomach." Without placing the woman at the lineage shrine, a soul might not "find the path" to enter her.[1]

Sex, Blood, and Birth

The symbolic language of "Holding Out the Spoon" emphasizes the link between reproduction and land. But Ehing believe there are two aspects to the creation of a child. A child is not only created from a soul but from the "blood" (*munya*) of men and women, which is mixed in sexual intercourse.

As a result of this mixture of substances, a child is consanguineously related to both parents, each of whom may refer to the child as "my blood." In light of this notion of blood, an individual expresses sexual incapacity because of age by saying "my blood is finished, my children received it all." Apart from blood, some persons also mentioned to me that a woman has "eggs," which when broken produce her period and when depleted cause infertility. One of my most perspicacious informants, however, insisted that this statement should be taken as a figurative expression.

Once a woman has conceived, the couple continue sexual activity until shortly before birth, for the developing child "nurses" on the blood of intercourse. For that reason the people claim that when a husband is absent, whether on a voyage or because of divorce, the woman carries the child longer than would have been the case had the child been properly "nourished."

When a woman is pregnant for the first time, she participates in a ritual called Bufine. *Bufine* means "to cover the upper body with a cloth," when, for example, it is cold or when one tries to ward off mosquitoes. In the ritual, a husband's sister brings a cloth and simply wraps it around her brother's wife. Nothing is necessarily said. The cloth is positioned so that it pushes down on the wife's breasts. The people say that a woman's breasts are "hard," that they are like there is "a broken piece of pot" inside, and that, if the cloth does not push down, the baby will not be able to nurse. Bufine, traditionally, was the first time a woman wore clothing on the upper part of her body. The cloth, by covering the developing woman, hides the sight of pregnancy from men.

Like the ritual of "Holding Out the Spoon," the rite of Bufine also serves to place a child in his father's house. Since the husband's sister shares his Kahin, "when she does Bufine, the soul knows that he is in the house of someone whom *his* child fathered." In other words, when she marries, a wife is first placed at the Kahin, in "Holding Out the Spoon", and then the child she is carrying is enveloped, one might say, by a woman of that Kahin.

The "covering" of pregnancy that is implied in the rite of Bufine is also conveyed linguistically. When Ehing describe a pregnant woman, they say she has a "stomach." There is no word (that I know of) which refers to a human womb, though there is a term (*kabian*) for the womb of an animal. These people know, of course, that a woman has a womb, but the language serves the rules of separation governed by Odieng.

Ehing also associate carrying a child with intestines (*mula*). A woman who gives birth may say "the child came out of my intestines." Women may insult a peer who has not become pregnant with "she eats all the time but defecates everything out." Hence, references to intestines are found among the taboos of Odieng, an elaboration of the rule that youth should not have any knowledge of birth.

The people perceive childbirth as a dangerous activity. A pregnant woman is "sick," and Ehing say that a woman who is about to deliver does not know whether she will live or die; when a woman gives birth, "her head enters near the earth" (the grave). In contrast to Kujamaat Diola women who give birth outside the compound, Ehing give birth in the woman's room of her husband's house (Sapir 1977: 4). Because of Odieng, I was prohibited from even getting near a delivery. But as I was also recognized as an outsider, several women, in deep privacy, did offer an account of one birth that occurred in a neighboring house. Here is what I was told: the young woman, who was giving birth for the first time, was very nervous. As a youth (*asunguru*), she had little or no idea of what was to happen. But now that she was in labor, the elder women in attendance informed her about some details of childbirth. And when told, apparently she shouted, "My sex will split open!" Then, she was reassured. "Yes, everyone's like that, even for the men at initiation. For us, it will split open, and the baby will come out. When it doesn't split open, the baby doesn't come out."

After delivering her first child, a woman is an "elder" (*abia*). For all births, she observes a set of taboos which are the same as those observed during menstruation.

1. The woman may not sit on a stool. She either sits on the ground or on an animal skin.
2. She may not sleep on a bed; she sleeps either on the ground or sometimes on a discarded door of the house.
3. She may not stand on the door sill of the house.
4. She cannot go up into her granary, separate rice from stalk, or stir rice in the family cooking pot.
5. She cannot enter any ponds, which, before the introduction of wells, were the source of drinking water.

Should a woman commit any of these acts, she will be caught by Odieng. The taboos during menstruation are terminated when the blood ceases. After birth, the taboos cease when Ehing perform a washing ritual—the name of which may be glossed "to resuscitate"—at a pond in the rice fields. A mother washes, shaves her head, and states "today I leave my taboos."

Forms of Marriage

In this account of marriage, I have stressed the walking of women in relation to the notions of souls. In other words, I have stressed the ideas that are inherent in sexual relations. Now I want to conclude this part of the soul's journey with a brief note about the structural dimensions of marriage—the rules that sociologically govern where a woman can and cannot move.

Ehing are organized into patronymic categories which are exogamous. Since the membership of these categories by definition includes that of an individual's House, a man is not allowed to marry any House sisters. But these rules of marriage are not coterminous with prohibitions on intercourse. It is forbidden to engage in sexual relations with a member of one's House. The people say it is *munyo* (to the best of my knowledge, there is no specific term that is equivalent to our use of the word "incest"). But sexual activity within the patronymic categories is not regarded as *munyo*.

A man may not marry any woman to whom he is connected by close female links. Specifically, he may not marry the daughter of his mother's sister or the daughter of his maternal grandmother's sister's daughter. The intent of the prohibitions, the people say, is to prevent conflict between "sisters" who would be expected to take opposing sides should their children's marriages run into trouble. Sororal polygyny is also forbidden. The roles of co-wives are thought to be fraught with difficulties, to which sisters should not be subject. Co-wives address each other by a term that was translated to me as "my enemy" (*abirindze*). To illustrate this relationship, I cannot resist recording the song a wife once composed about her peer:

> It resembles something without form
> It resembles an airplane
> When she dances, if you look out over her buttocks
> You face the village of Burefai [a village far away]

Outside these negative rules, an individual may marry any woman of his own or of several lower age-grades. The people say that it is good for a woman to marry within her natal village, for then she can easily visit her kin. Of the 132 marriages contracted by 66 adult men in Bakunum, roughly half were with women of the village.

Three forms of marriage have specific names: sister-exchange and marriages with each cross-cousin. When men exchange sisters (*bukio*), they still must offer gifts of wine. Although the people expressed approval of this mode of marriage, I recorded only three instances in Bakunum. It was pointed out to me that sister exchange can also complicate marital life: "If you treat your wife poorly, he can do the same to your sister."

Marriage with the mother's brother's daughter is called "receiving the maternal kin" (*baiyap kumumen*). In this form of marriage, an individual "inherits the door" of his father. Marriage with the daughter of a paternal aunt is called "righting the bed" (*keirin buna*). The word *keirin* is more literally glossed as to "stand upright," in the sense, for example, of being sick and then getting up (and well). The word is also used to denote the pot in the house where drinking water is stored; the pot is round at the bottom but topped with a long, upright neck, the feature that gives it its name. The sense this word has in marriage, according to Ehing, is that a woman who goes to produce children for another House compensates by sending her own daughter back in marriage. As one elder put it, in this way women "put back the seed."

Death and the Soul

Up to this point in our account of the movement of the soul, we have seen how Ehing communicate the falling of souls into women. Now it is time to look at the other side of this movement—when the soul moves back into the earth. That part of the journey is expressed in death ritual.

The pairing of marriage and death rituals is rooted in a metaphysic in which life and death are mutually defining events. The people themselves make this point and tell a story that drives it home. The first people, I was told, once held a meeting and apparently decided, with the powers that such mythical first people often possess, that death would no longer take so many people. And so death ceased. But after that decision, "a person did not fall as *agun*"—that is, there were no more births. So the people returned to God and said "the women we are marrying are not becoming pregnant." And God answered, "You said you didn't want people to die; but when a person dies, he comes back again, you give birth to him. Now, if you want that, let the old die. When they have died, the women will become pregnant."

Mortuary rituals among the Ehing are complex and elaborate events. My aim here is not to describe these rituals in their entirety, for not only are the ceremonies filled with detail, but there are many variations as well. A man's funeral, for example, differs from a woman's, as do funerals of the old from funerals of the young. Again, special rites may be performed for a man who was the head of a shrine, a prodigious tapper of wine, or a renowned hunter. Rather than describe all of this rich material here, I will concentrate on the features of the rites that are always performed and that, in this sense, constitute their elemental action.

The key feature I want to point out is the path of the soul, and to show this path I pay most attention to the position of the corpse. Ehing represent the passage of the soul as a duration of time, and this time is marked and the soul is moved through a series of actions which position the body farther and farther from the houses of the living. The movement of the body is a metaphor of the soul's journey.[2]

A death in a village is announced by the wails of women. Though some persons may quickly walk toward the noise and inquire into the identity of the deceased, most villagers hear by word of mouth and do not arrive at the house of the dead until evening of the day of death.

Ehing say that a dead person is someone who has become "dry." The dead are dry first of all because the soul has departed, which makes the "blood dry"; the soul and blood are intrinsically connected in death as well as in procreation. The soul that has left the body to become *afuga* is the "right" soul, the true soul, which is always invisible. Although the departure of the right soul is thought tantamount to death, Ehing also say the body itself may become dry gradually—for example, the legs can "dry up" first and become rigid before the rest of the body.

This is the primary sense in which dryness of the body is associated with loss of life. Additionally, however, the body is literally drained of fluid during the night after death. As villagers gather at the deceased's house, the body is carried from the room where the person expired and out through the rear door of the house. The body is carried out naked, except for a cloth covering the genital region, and propped up in a sitting position against some palm fronds placed at the back or side wall of the house. It is positioned over a hole dug in the terrace which catches any discharge from the anus throughout the night. Once the deceased has been properly arranged at the wall, a sister's son libates some wine at the side of the corpse, pouring the wine in the general direction of the hole. He then cuts a chicken's neck at the same place, holding the bird firmly so that it does not move as it dies. One bundle of paddy is brought from the deceased's granary; the cluster is split in half and hung on pegs placed in the wall next to the shoulders of the body. This shows, according to one comment, that the deceased "ate good things"—that is, rice and not persons (the food of witches). The body remains in position throughout the night, and members of the village stand watch and sing until morning. If the deceased is a woman, her friends spend their time spinning cotton, work associated with females.

Toward daybreak, the body is taken down and lain face down into the hole so that a fluid Ehing call *kalo* spills out. Ehing believe that *kalo* is in the spinal column and that it also fills the brain; *kalo* is to be distinguished from blood, although it is sometimes bloody, which Ehing interpret as a sign that "someone has killed the person."

The funeral proper takes place the day after death. Early in the morning the cadaver is taken away from the wall and washed, usually by the sister's children of the same sex as the deceased. Cotton is put in its ears and mouth; its legs are tied together, and it is wrapped in cloth. The cadaver is then placed on a stretcher made from palm fronds and sticks of wood taken from the meander, the waterway at the boundary of the village. The cadaver is positioned on its stomach, with its arms folded back so that the wrists are tucked under its chin as if to hold up the head. The body is tied and supported in this position by strips of cotton supplied by the deceased's sisters; cloth is then placed over its face and the rest of the figure is wrapped in traditional indigo cloth. Finally, a cap, often red, is placed on top of its head.

When these preparations have been completed, maternal kin provide wine which is libated at the side of the stretcher. The wine is said to "sweep the face" of the deceased, to make his vision as an *afuga* (soul) unclouded, so that he will be able in the underground to determine the cause of his own death.

The stretcher is then taken out of the rear courtyard and brought to the front of the house. The path taken is significant. Instead of carrying the body through the house and out the front door, the stretcher-bearers

Fig. 4.1. At funerals, women dance with baskets and tools associated with their work.

break a hole in the fence at the side of the house and carry the body around to the front door. There the cadaver rests, surrounded by women and by baskets of its own rice, called "rice at the head of the cadaver." Kin and friends may supplement this rice with their own bundles. After the funeral this rice will be pounded and eaten by the married female kin of the deceased's lineage.

The funeral dances (Fig. 4.1) begin about noon and continue until late in the afternoon when the ceremony begins. The mounted cadaver is picked up by two men, known as "carriers of the cadaver," and taken away from the door and out into the front courtyard. It is to be addressed and questioned by kin and friends, who position themselves in the doorway of the house. The actual speaker at any one moment takes several steps forward to meet the cadaver, which is held high in front of him. If the deceased is a man, speakers include his brothers, wives, maternal kin, children, and perhaps close friends. If a woman, they include her husband, perhaps his lineage kin, her agnates, and her children. When a man goes out to meet the cadaver and speak, he carries a bottle of wine which he spills on the ground intermittently as he talks. When women address the dead, they carry a small container of pounded rice which they spill as an offering. Usually some of these speakers twirl a chicken around the head of the cadaver as they talk and then kill it by pounding it on the ground. If by chance the chicken should touch the corpse, an *ahula* (non-initiate) cannot share its meat.

As a relative talks to the cadaver (Fig. 4.2), it dances in the court-yard—from our point of view, the men carrying the body dance. It moves forward or backward or sometimes circles—all in response to the speeches it hears. In these speeches, relatives recall the illness that led to death, promise the sacrifices that will be made on the deceased's behalf (or apologize for the fact that not enough animals will be killed). And they ask the dead, "Did someone kill you?"—an allusion to witchcraft.

This practice warrants a brief explanation. While funerals for the old are joyous events with jubilant dances—for they have lived full lives and left many children—those for children and adults in midlife are always associated with witchcraft, *mota*. In Ehing thought, a witch is someone who out of jealousy causes harm to others. They do so by roaming about at night to eat "dirty things," that is, the souls of other persons. Ehing hold that these victims of witchcraft, once they move underground, will try to seek retribution. Now, in the context of the funeral, the questioning of the cadaver not only revolves around whether he or she is a victim of witchcraft, but also whether he or she is a victim of retribution. The deaths of the old and the very young tend to escape this suspicion, but

Fig. 4.2. At funerals, relatives question the deceased (on stretcher) and interpret the response.

those of young and middle-age adults are invariably subject to gossip: did the deceased do something in the past? The more shocking the death, especially deaths caused by accidents, the more likely that people will think during the funeral about the possibilities of a victim seeking revenge. In one instance, when a youth died when a tree fell on him, people even thought back to the death of a young girl several years before and speculated that it was she who at last had achieved revenge. The year she died, the youth, Lambert, had had a bumper cash crop of peanuts. Soon after Lambert's funeral, I heard stories that Lambert might have sold her soul to a bush spirit in return for supernatural help with his crop. Snake bites are also thought to be retribution. Ehing believe snakes bite only when acting on behalf of an *afuga* seeking revenge. Anyone who dies of snakebite is buried without clothes as a sign of his status as a witch.

When asked during the funeral about the circumstances of death, the cadaver responds "no" to statements in the speeches by moving backward or circling, but interest is riveted on the "yes" responses. For then the cadaver lunges forward and tries to re-enter the house. It is blocked there by the entire group of speakers and relatives who raise up their arms against it.

The dramatic message is clear. Once dead, the body is not allowed back into the front of the house. For that reason it was carried, the night before, into the front court through a hole in the fence. The movement away from the house has begun.

After the speeches, the body is set down in the front courtyard and surrounded by women, while men attend to the work of sacrifice. The sacrifice takes place at the Kahin, the lineage shrine. In theory, one bull should be sacrificed, though there may sometimes be a supplementary bull or a pig. The bull is provided by the deceased's agnates. The animal is held up off the ground by several planks of wood, and its neck is cut so that the blood spills down onto the spirit.

Ehing have told me that the "soul" of this animal is used to pay a "curer" in the underworld so that the deceased may learn the cause of his death: "When he arrives in the earth, his face (vision) will be clear." Although some informants stated that it is the *afuga* (deceased) himself who seeks the aid of a curer, others stated that this is the responsibility of the souls of maternal kin, who provide assistance "below" just as they do in village life.

After the sacrifice, the deceased is taken in a procession toward the grave.[3] Adult men and women are usually buried in the lineage's cemetery adjacent to the houses, but persons who died before marrying are buried in the rear courtyard of a house. There does not seem to be a hard and fast rule here, for I saw a very old father's sister buried in the yard of her brother's son. The traditional Ehing grave is circular for the first several feet below ground and then opens into a deeper rectangular hollow, but these days most graves are simply rectangular. At graveside, elders remove the corpse from the stretcher. Sisters' children remove several of the indigo cloths used to cover the corpse, but the face of the cadaver remains covered. At this point discussion invariably breaks out about which cloths should be left on the body to cover it in the tomb and which will be claimed by relatives.

The body is lowered into and placed in the grave by a ritual specialist (a "digger"). He enters the tomb with a ritual knife—a threat, according to my informants, to show the deceased what would happen if he or she tried to avoid burial. Death begins the transformation of *da* to *afuga,* and Ehing perceive that the former state is not relinquished complacently. The deceased is importuned to remain inanimate in the grave and not to become a "zombie" (*nyazango*).

The body is laid on its right side, with the right hand tucked under its ear and with its legs extended. Men are laid in an east-west direction, I was told, "to face the rice fields," although villages and fields are not laid out with such geographical regularity; women are laid out in north-south orientation.

For some time after an individual's death, Ehing will not publicly pronounce his or her name. And others who shared the same name will often change theirs after the funeral.

Again, in this abbreviated description of the funeral, I want to stress the movement of the body. It is moved away from the house by a series of steps: from room to outside wall, to the front of the house, to burial in the rear courtyard or cemetery. The point is that this movement represents stages in the journey of the soul.

The Homecoming of Souls

The final rituals that express this journey of the soul occur several months later, and in these the movement from *da* to *afuga* is finally completed. These are called Kazo Odieng and Kazo Esuum. The word *kazo* means "to strike in a downward motion"—as, for example, when a chicken pecks at grain. In these rituals various objects—headed by the hatchet (*odieng*) or weaving knife (*esuum*)—are used to mark the separation of the living from the dead. The ritual itself takes place in the rear courtyard of the house, directly against the fence. For this occasion, the fence is supported with wood brought from the meander. The participants sit on a mat with their backs to the fence and with their faces toward the rice fields.

The form, if not the details, of the rituals is the same for men and women. An elder positions himself behind the persons on the mat, and a sister's child (*asebun*) squats down at the base of their extended legs. The ritual of "Striking Down With the Hatchet" begins when the brothers and sisters of the deceased pass the long handle of their brother's hoe under and over their legs and, finally, hold it against their foreheads. The elder then passes the deceased's hatchet across each of their heads, brushing downward against the handle. While doing so, he says, "Here is the hatchet of your brother; today it's finished." The elder then "strikes down" with the small lance used in tapping wine, with a yam, and with a taro. He then blows in the right and left ears of each person. Immediately afterwards, the sister's child runs his hands—"sweeping"—down the ankles of those sitting, and says "go home to the rice fields." The brothers and sisters then leave the mat and are replaced by the deceased's children, and the ritual is repeated.

In Kazo Esuum, for a woman, the detail of the fulcrum shovel is omitted. The elder brushes the heads of the brothers, sisters, and children with a weaving knife, an instrument used to spin cotton, a piece of raw cotton, and a bead. With each object, the officiant repeats the same statement: "Here is the knife of your sister; today it's finished"; and a sister's daughter sweeps the legs with the same admonition to "go home."

There is much to say about this rite,[4] but in this context I want to focus on its final action. In sending the deceased to the fields, the sister's child completes the movement of a soul. In the funeral we saw how this movement is presented through an idiom of space. The body is moved from inside to outside the house and is not allowed to reenter; the burial occurs farther away, in the courtyard; and now the final ceremonies take place at the edge of the yard, against the surrounding fence. Moreover, this edge of the courtyard is symbolically the edge of the village, for the fence is supplemented with wood brought from the meander, the natural boundary of a village. At this boundary of village space, the soul is at last totally separated from its kin and completes its journey. Leaving all space associated with above ground, it goes "home." And from these fields, it will be reborn.

Ehing say that sometimes a person who was a witch may be refused by his lineage's souls (*kufuga*). When he arrives in the earth, his dead ancestors "strike" him, forcing him to flee, and this too produces a "zombie" (*nyazango*). These creatures travel at night, making sounds like a hyena, with arms that stretch down to the ground; they try to enter your house in ill-will. Zombies represent a short-circuit in the cycle of souls; they will not become *afuga* and therefore cannot be reborn. A zombie, I was told, can only become an *afuga* if eaten by a hyena.

The Meaning of the Tale

I began my interpretation of Ehing sexual categories with the question of why a woman must move in marriage. The answer now can be stated quite directly. a woman moves because of the souls. I want to stress this cycle of souls as a fundamental concept of Ehing culture.

Because of souls, the movement of women, in contrast to the locality of men who build houses, is the idiom that orders the notion of descent. It is because a woman moves to the man's Kahin, to give birth in his house, that the soul "falling into" her body is one of the man's ancestors now reborn. In the marriage myth, the woman's shelter had to be replaced by the house. It had to be replaced because the movement of a man rather than a woman would have been tantamount to matrilineal rather than patrilineal descent.

Because of the souls, also, we can understand more fully certain structural features of the House. Earlier, I remarked on the shallow range of genealogical knowledge within a House. This feature, we now can understand, is dictated by the cycle of souls and names. The names beyond the time of grandfathers do not, in fact, go back in time; these are the names not of ancestors but of children.

It is also the cycle of souls that informs the ritual action during the harvest rite of Ihin. In the last chapter I described how, at Ihin, children gather to eat the newly harvested rice. Now we can see that, when elders bring the new crop and the children to the Kahin, they may well be said to be celebrating the harvest of souls as well as of rice. This celebration is what Ehing mean most profoundly when they say, "Kahin and land are one."

5

Initiation

At the outset of this study, I suggested that the separation of the sexes is pivotal to the structure of Ehing society. With that point in mind, it might seem that the materials presented in the last chapters are tangential to my primary problem. For, although I have described Ehing notions of male-female relations, this description seems so far to have focused on the union rather than the separation of the sexes. What I have shown is that notions of men's locality and women's "walking," of land and Kahin, are all central to reproduction. But apart from an oblique allusion to Odieng in the marriage text, where the woman chases away the man because "he wants to see what I do," the spirit seems to be conspicuously absent.

In fact, this impression is not an accurate one. To the contrary, Odieng's rules are deeply implicated in the notions of Houses, souls, and male rights. This work of the spirit is most visible in the initiation that Ehing call Kombutsu. In this ritual, youth become adults and in this way continue the cycle of souls in social terms. But even more importantly, in Kombutsu Odieng links the rights of men to the powers of women. Through its rules of separation, such as the rule that separates youth from corpses and especially the rule that keeps women from the initiation, the spirit orders the most fundamental ideas that define a House.

Ehing openly proclaim that Kombutsu is their largest and most important ritual. It is altogether an extraordinary event. In part, it is extraordinary because it is a time when the whole of Ehing society is governed by Odieng: the power, of most of the other spirits in the cosmos are suspended when the youth enter the forest. The red color of Odieng is the color of Kombutsu. It is the color of the blood that falls from the youth as they are circumcised. In part, also, Kombutsu is so striking because of its timing. The ritual occurs in a cycle of approximately twenty-five years. The event I record here occurred in 1979, and I was most fortunate to have been able to return to Senegal at that time to see this part of Odieng's work.

What follows is a lengthy account of the ritual. Although there is a regional literature on Diola initiation in the Casamance, much of it refers to general themes rather than to detailed descriptions of particular rites (Girard 1969; Thomas 1965). In the account that I provide here, I leave any comparative questions and concerns aside. My interest lies solely in the meaning of Kombutsu in a particular system of social ideas.

Preliminaries

Kombutsu is one in a cycle of male initiations linked, the people say, to those of the Edii and Arame peoples in Guinea-Bissau. The Ehing are supposed to perform their ritual the year following that of the Edii and the Arame after the Ehing. But elders also say that the timing of Kombutsu depends on the growth of a special termite hill. Every year men from five designated Houses, and I believe only those men whose children are already initiated, libate at a secret clearing and observe whether the hill can be seen. Plans for the initiation are said to begin the year the hill is visible. A large dance in 1972 announced the coming of this past initiation, and elders stated at that time that "the fan palm leaf has fallen," a circumlocution for the real sign which they had seen. I was once told that the termite hill grows year after year until the elders can see a "knife of iron" emerge ("float") out of the ground; in any case, they will tell other important elders that "the knife is ripe" (ready).[1]

On the basis of the cycle of rituals and these signs, an initiation was to have occurred in 1978. Because the rains of the previous year were poor, however, Ehing decided that their stocks of rice were insufficient to feed all the expected visitors; they postponed the ritual.

In December of 1978, the men from each village gathered in the clearing at the grand Odieng to consider again the performance of Kombutsu. They each gave a large pot of wine to Sisa Sagna, who serves as intermediary between populace and spirit, and who is the *amanya,* the ritual director of Kombutsu. Sisa remarked, as the scene was later described to me, that unlike the year before when the rains had been bad, this year the rains had been plentiful and there was an abundant crop. He then turned to the villagers to ask if they were certain that he should offer wine to the spirit, that he should seal a compact to hold Kombutsu with a libation. With their affirmation, he prayed to the spirit: "The Ehing are here today, and you have heard as they have spoken. The children are grown; this year we go wash them." Shortly after this visit to the spirit, it rained—a rarity for December—and this was taken as an especially auspicious sign.

Kombutsu in 1979

In May, the men returned to Odieng to set an actual date for Kombutsu. Sisa called for those assembled to be quiet, and Bunesi Nyafouna, an elder of Bakunum, was the first to propose a date: June 28. Someone from Bafikan then countered that this was "too close" and other villages joined in the discussion, some supporting Bakunum and others Bafikan. One of the questions raised concerned children who were away at high schools, and the schedule of their examinations at the end of the year. An elder from Bakunum said they had considered that problem and, in a typical bargaining ploy, suggested the earlier date of June 22, a move which made their original proposal seem more reasonable. The 28th it was, and Sisa, asking the group "are you sure?" poured wine onto the shrine: "Ehing said we count four weeks, and then the next *ozalum* will be Kombutsu." *Ozalum* is a day of the week, and the day on which Kombutsu must occur. Sisa also added in his libation that "we are tired of saying *munyo* to the children," meaning that after Kombutsu the elders will no longer have to hide things from so many youth. Although the people were holding this Kombutsu in June, traditionally the ritual occurred in April, before the onset of the work season. Nowadays, throughout the Casamance, groups have adapted to the demands of the school year and to governmental pressure.

Throughout the year I had been following these events as best I could through letters from Mossi Bassene, my elder "brother." In early January 1979, Mossi informed me of the December meeting to alert me to make preparations to come. In April I heard from him again, and at that time he indicated only that Kombutsu was to be held in June. This news was the last I heard before leaving for Senegal. Thus, when my wife and I arrived back in Dakar in mid-June—the earliest arrival our obligations would allow—we were anxious about our timing. With the kind help of Professor Abdoulaye Diop and the officials of l'Institut Fondamental d'Afrique Noire, we were able to proceed as quickly as possible to Ziguinchor. Once there, moments after dropping our bags at our hotel, I walked over to a Total gas station where I knew an Ehing worked. Finding him, I learned that, though some preparations had begun, we were in good time for Kombutsu. In three days we were back in Bakunum.

We took up residence in a room in Mossi's house and started to accustom ourselves once again to village routine. Mossi and his wife, Maget, kept talking about all the "strangers" who would visit during the ritual, about how the hallway and veranda would be crowded with people. The talk made us feel a little territorial about our small space. In anticipation of these guests, the women in the villages had been pounding rice and making palm-oil sauce for several weeks. Many households also had purchased large (100-kilogram) sacks of rice from Ziguinchor to make sure there would be enough to feed both the visitors during Kombutsu and themselves for the rest of the summer.

During these initial days at Bakunum I heard more fully the details of the meetings which had fixed the date of the initiation. Also during this time several fathers approached me to ask about medicines that might help protect and heal their children's wounds. To ask, they led me away from the house lest a youth or woman overhear the conversation. Some merchants arrived to sell gunpowder, and the normally conservative men purchased fifty boxes at 1,800 francs each (then about $10.00) from just one of these, a Diola who sold his wares out of Mossi's house.

Secrecy and Witnesses

Kombutsu is a highly secret and serious ritual, and not at all something that outsiders, particularly white outsiders, would normally observe. Certainly they might be invited to the public meals and festivities, where women are allowed as well, but their entrance into the bush would be blocked. In 1976, when the Bayot held their Kombutsu, I had gone in the company of Mossi and Apa Sagna to the house of one of their Bayot friends, where we ate a fine meal of rice and meat. After the meal, when everyone moved toward the sacred bush where the cutting was to take place, my presence was challenged. At one point I was chased away with a machete. My Ehing friends were almost as upset as I was, and in going home that day they kept talking about how I would surely be invited to their Kombutsu.

When I returned to Senegal, I was nevertheless uneasy about the problem of secrecy. My apprehension stemmed from what I had later learned about my episode with the Bayot: those who had chased me away most vehemently were not Bayot at all but visiting guests—specifically, members of the Bandial-Diola group who live just north of the Ehing-Bayot area. In some sense, it was strangers and not hosts who had overseen the secrecy of the ritual, and I was inquiet about whether they might try to do the same with the Ehing event.

An initiation, it became plain, is a regional event, an event performed in various cycles and in differing forms throughout the Casamance and Guinea-Bissau. For this initiation, the Ehing were hosting "strangers" from several groups of Diola, and from Edii and Arame. Though many of these people could not understand the local dialect, they could understand the meaning of the initiation, and they formed its community. The strangers were coming to celebrate the initiation, but, more than that, they were coming as its audience. I gained the strong impression that the visitors were present to make certain that the ritual would be performed properly; as witnesses to the event, they also gained a moral power to influence its direction.

My concern about seeing Kombutsu, therefore, had less to do with the Ehing people themselves than with their relationship to these strangers. Would the visitors balk at my attendance? And if they did, would Bakunum, collectively, be able to face them down? For my part, I took what precautions I could. As soon as I arrived in the village, I made known my intention to provide a bull to be killed in honor of Kombutsu and in honor of Bakunum. The initiation is one of the major ritual occasions when cattle are killed, and I wanted to contribute to the celebration. But to be more fully honest, I also made this offer to steel the fortitude of Bakunum. The village was indeed extremely pleased. On June 23, Mossi arranged for me to give 40,000 francs to Robert Sagna, who, with several of his friends, was to travel the next day among Diola villages to seek a suitable animal.

The following day, however, Robert returned empty-handed. The bull that he had seen was, in his view, too small for the money. My bull would wait, the village decided, until later in the summer when, with the guests gone, all Bakunum could enjoy the meat themselves. In the meantime, the village kept the money in their collective fund.

Perhaps the bull would not have been needed, perhaps the bull alone would have been enough, but my position became greatly strengthened through an unexpected, if typically African, source: kinship. Three days before Kombutsu was to begin, Mossi received an early guest, a rugged but quiet man about forty years old. It was his brother who had come from Edii in Guinea-Bissau. He and Mossi are related through a common paternal grandfather, for Mossi's father had been born in Edii and had later emigrated to Bakunum. In the next few days I learned that Subati held a political position in the swampy region of Guinea-Bissau from which he came, and he seemed naturally to command respect. During the day of Kombutsu, Subati became my escort. I still do not know if Mossi had asked him to, or if he tacitly assumed the role. Nothing was ever said to me, but as I walked with the villagers, strangers, and initiates toward the sacred scene in the bush where the secret cutting was performed, he walked step by step with me through the crowd, and he stood with me, pointing out this and that, during the entire ceremony. His presence made my own unassailable.

Ritual Preparations

As busy as the people were in mid-June preparing for their guests, their religious preparations for Kombutsu were even more demanding. When I arrived, there was evidence everywhere of recent rituals: shrines had been cleared of weeds, there were broken pieces of pot next to them, special shrines for particular rites of passage had been recently set up and just as recently abandoned. These preparations were guided by two principles. The first is that during Kombutsu the society comes under the governance of only three spirits: Odieng, a spirit call Kahus (which protects the initiates in the bush), and the Kahin. All other spirits had to be "abandoned." In practical terms, this meant that anyone who had ever asked a spirit to avenge some wrong was required to lift this curse. In the Ehing idiom, anyone who had placed a "hand" at a spirit was required to "dig" it up. Otherwise, the spirit might catch an initiate during Kombutsu, an initiate who himself might be innocent of any wrongdoing. A spirit, when asked to work vengeance, will often attack a relative of the perpetrator rather than himself. Unless all curses were lifted, therefore, "a child in the bush might be punished for a misdeed of his father."

The second principle is that before youth enter the bush, they must participate in all the rituals of the life cycle which would normally have been performed as they came of age. The days, then, were tightly scheduled with rites of passage. For the very young, these rituals would include Ibun, a hair-cutting ceremony called Kamis, and Ichin, a ritual described to me as the "small Kombutsu." Furthermore, had the parents of any youth recently died, the final mortuary ceremonies of Kazo Odieng or Kazo Esuum were immediately performed. Like the arrangements made before an extended journey, all spiritual affairs were being set in order.

Of all these ceremonies, only Ichin bears directly on the symbolism and meaning of Kombutsu. Associated with the spirit Echin, whose shrine is found in each village, Ichin normally is performed every four years and is accompanied by many public festivities and dances. But in 1979, Ichin was held privately and out of its cycle in order to ready the very youngest children in the village who were to participate in Kombutsu. In the afternoon of the appointed day and before any children were brought to the shrine, an elder killed a rooster over a small hole which had been dug next to Echin, letting the blood spill within. Then, once the rooster had died, the elder placed its head in the hole, pushing it down into the earth so that it was partly buried. In the evening the children were brought to the shrine and one by one they were placed face down over the hole. Two elders softly sang the secret song of Ichin in the ears of each:

> Wo *Echin* dances on the back y-i-i-i
> Our elder taps his ritual stick, it's finished.

After singing the song, one of the elders tapped the back of the child's head with a stick which had been stained with the blood of the rooster. Then each initiate was given a handful of rice within which was hidden a small raw piece of the rooster's liver. The children were told to swallow the rice quickly. Finally, they were carried out of the clearing on elders' shoulders and washed with water. To the youth the song and symbolism of Ichin are inscrutable, and, according to elders, they are meant to be so. Ichin prefigures Kombutsu: the blood of the rooster prefigures the blood the initiates themselves will spill. As the youth face their future, they must do so without any comprehension, for foreknowledge of Kombutsu is prohibited by Odieng.

Two locations in a village are the setting for the major events of Kombutsu. One is a patch of woods right in the middle of the rice fields. Reserved for ritual, this bush has never been cleared. Each village gives its wood a proper name, but all refer to these areas as places where one "dresses"—an ironic description, as these sacred woods are where one stands naked.

The second location involves the Kahus spirit. The role of this spirit in Kombutsu is to watch over and protect the youths during their period of seclusion. Each village has a Kahus spirit, whose shrine is located within a tract of upland bush some distance from the village houses. The paths leading to the Kahus shrines are marked off by curtains of leaves that warn women not to enter the area. In any village the elder responsible for Kahus is one on whose land the spirit is found; in Bakunum this is Bunesi Nyafouna, of House Bazolo. As priest of Kahus, he played a major role in that village's Kombutsu.

About ten days before the ritual, the initiated men in each village began to build wood-framed huts next to the Kahus shrine. A lineage with many children constructed its own, separate hut, but smaller groups pooled their labor and shared a dwelling. The initial construction took about four days; the men then waited several days before covering the huts with fan-palm leaves. Once the men finished the huts, they made a fence of leaves around the shrine itself, for though initiates would sleep in proximity to the spirit, they were forbidden to see the shrine. Another fence around the entire area of huts screened activities from the eyes of any women who dared to pry.

During this work, Apa Sagna, a middle-aged man whose skill at carving often drew him commissions to make hoes, carved out two drums from a log. These drums were at Kahus that summer, and after Kombutsu, they would become the drums played at village funerals. On June 20, the village killed a bull; its skin was used to cover the drums. When they held the animal over the Kahus and cut its neck, they held its mouth shut tight so that it could not cry out. As it was butchered, part of its neck was removed and placed at the shrine, signifying, I soon learned, the captured voice of the animal which was transferred to the spirit. And from there, in turn, the voice was transferred to the "master of the forest" (apia kalu).

The "master of the forest" is represented by a wooden instrument, freshly carved for each Kombutsu and shaped like a knife. The blade was about 20 to 30 centimeters in length and four notches were carved into each of its sides; its handle was short and stubby. A lengthy cord was attached to the handle; traditionally, the cotton for the cord was prepared either by a girl who had not yet menstruated, or a woman past menopause. When the instrument was finished (June 22), Bunesi took it to the Kahus, where during his libation "the voice of the bull" was transferred. He then sacrificed a rooster at the shrine, dripped its blood over the Kahus and the instrument, and prayed for the well-being of Kombutsu. When it was time to try the "master," Amain Sagna, an elder of House Buzenu, was the first to take hold of the cord and whip the instrument around in a circle. It was only then that I realized that the "master" was a bull-roarer and that, quite literally, the men had given it the captured voice of the bull. Amain Sagna, however, only managed to produce a sound of rustled air. Others then tried spinning in one direction and then the next, with one hand and then another, but that day no one had any success in producing the desired voice.

Two days later, the men tried again. In the meantime, Apa had made the blade thinner. Eventually, as if the instrument were reawakening to some long lost ability, it began to make a faint whir. As the men became more proficient, its voice gradually became stronger, and it would be heard throughout the nights of Kombutsu.

On June 26, men gathered small, black termite hills and transported these to the grove in the rice fields. That night, the men in each of the villages walked from house to house to gather wine, which later would be served to visitors, and rice, which would be eaten during the first days of Kombutsu. Each father contributed a measure of rice for every child who would participate in the ritual, and each lineage gathered its paddy in one large basket. Traditionally, each father was also to have offered a ten-liter bowl of wine, but this year, as Kombutsu was held toward the end of the wine season, most men contributed less. At every house on the tour a few rifles were fired.

The next morning, elders of each House gathered to discuss which animals they would kill in honor of Kombutsu. Cattle are the proper victims, and, by the end of the entire ritual late in August, some Houses had sacrificed as many as fifteen head. It was expected that any individual who owned a beast would volunteer it, but some, like Apa Seba, the eldest member of House Kula, had made known that they were not about to offer their own bulls. Instead, the members of Kula had bought a small bull to kill.

In the afternoon, animals were killed and butchered in preparation for the following day. Toward dusk, the youth were shaved in the courtyard of each House. All the initiates had their heads shaved, but a few were shaved under their arms as well. Overly attentive to this sign of their changing status, I asked one barber what was to be done with the hair piling up on the ground? As I had suggested a point of tradition, he ran at once to an elder, who shrugged and replied, "Nothing. We'll throw it in the bush." When the shaving was over, elders and youth marched in procession to the village dance ground. There the younger women of the village sang and clapped as the initiates danced, and their excitement was palpable.

Wrestling the Heron

In Bakunum, all told there were 112 initiates, and these ranged in age from about eighteen months to their mid-twenties. Even though the initiation would be difficult, fathers were anxious to induct their youngest children if at all possible rather than to have them wait another twenty-five years to become "elders" (abia). Those who would remain youth (ahula) would be like "beasts who know nothing; they can't see cadavers or care for sick parents."

It is Kombutsu that determines the ritual rights of an elder and not chronological age, a point graphically illustrated by the plight of a man in another village who had missed the previous initiation and so had had, for all this time and in spite of his gray beard, the ritual status of a child.

Two rules govern participation in the ritual. First, a father and son cannot become elders at the same time. Second, a person must be initiated in the same village as was his father. Thus, fathers who had moved away from their natal villages brought their sons back for Kombutsu. Otherwise, the son could never eat or drink in that village again.

Although a few visitors trickled into Bakunum the night of the 27th, the majority arrived the next morning. The Edii and Arame peoples had walked since the middle of the night from their homes in Guinea-Bissau. The visitors arrived in small groups—the women in fine cloth, the men carrying spears, rifles, or machetes—and each group knew precisely which Ehing was to be its host. Bakunum must have received four hundred visitors that day, doubling the size of the village.

During the morning people wandered about the village, stopping here and there to converse or to share a little wine. But by noon, the visitors assembled at various houses to eat the meal of rice and meat which inaugurated the events of the day. After the meal, Kombutsu finally began.

The youth of each House were led to a secluded spot where they were stripped of their clothing and washed with a mixture of water and a plant called *busan*. Each initiate was given two cloths, a black and white striped cloth which he wore around his waist and a dark indigo cloth which he wore draped over his head. The mothers of the initiates spun the thread for these, and also paid for their weaving. The initiates were then led by the elders to the Kahin where a libation was held:

> This year the palm leaf has fallen. You see how the children are gathered here. When we libate here for them, we libate for *mazunemi* ("well-being"). We go with them. We go and will return with *mazunemi*. No one will be missed, we did not find that with our fathers. Our fathers did not say, "when you go wash a child, he'll be lost." That's *munyo*.

A note of explication. The elder here referred to Kombutsu as a "washing," just as Sisa did at the earlier libation at the grand Odieng. This reference at the Kahin is meant as circumlocution, for women and youth may listen to the libation. The term Kombutsu itself gives no hint that the ritual involves a circumcision; it is simply the proper name for this initiation. Whenever elders describe or refer to Kombutsu in public contexts or within earshot of children, they say that on that day a heron descends in the guise of a person in order to wrestle with the initiates. In anticipation of this event, male children are instructed to always refer to

the heron, *nyamero,* as "papa." They should respect the bird. They are told
that if they were to call the bird *nyamero,* the heron will strike them as they
enter Kombutsu. Ehing girls, on the other hand, may call *nyamero* by its
name or "papa." They do not always abide by the respect shown by boys;
in banter with boys, they may even insult the bird. I find the sense of these
insults elusive; three examples: "he defecates fish!," "he has dry legs!,"
"long back of head!" In turn boys may respond, "*Nyamero,* you don't
know him. When he has descended on the day of Kombutsu, if you look
you won't recognize him."

After the libation, initiates and elders, while singing, walked in a
small circle around the living area of the House. They then moved out of
the circle—the initiates had been led in a circle, I was told, as a gesture of
delay, for one does not move quickly toward the moment of Kombutsu—
to a path used only during this ritual which leads toward the rice fields. As
the group left the House's area, strangers at the rear, holding sticks and old
rifles, formed a guard to push back the singing and dancing women.
There is nothing subtle here about the separation of the sexes.

Singing as they marched, and with enthusiasts running off to the side
of the procession to fire a quick shot, the strangers and elders accompanied the initiates to the pasture land which lies at the border of upland
and rice fields. There, the Houses of the village converged, and all moved
across the fields to within a hundred yards or so of the sacred bush. The
initiates sat down on a long bund which is named *ovulelum* (from the verb
"undress"), and here their cloths were taken from them. In the meantime,
all the strangers went on ahead and entered the patch of sacred forest.

Quite suddenly, the eldest son of the elder responsible for the Kahus
spirit (in Bakunum, Bunesi's son Remi) was grabbed by the arm and run
toward the narrow path which leads into the bush. Hurdling the bunds,
he was told by an elder, "Don't fear. You're going to wrestle *nyamero.*"
Seconds after Bunesi's son started, others from the various Houses followed in quick order, and those of us who were not to be initiated scurried
toward the bush as well.

Breaking through the curtain of leaves which guards the path, an
initiate was first confronted with a mass of singing and dancing men. The
space inside the bush seemed too small for the crowd, but the initiates ran
on through the visitors who just barely cleared a space for them and
abruptly faced one of five or six strangers poised on all fours: the herons
who had descended in the guise of men. The strangers did not wear the
black coloring of the birds but the red of Kombutsu: most wore either a
red cap or shirt. Coming face to face with the squatting figures, some of
the initiates momentarily assumed a wrestling pose, in anticipation of a
match. Others, for just the briefest time, seemed stunned and unsure of

what to do. And then the heron pulled into the open the knife he was holding behind and cut off the foreskin of each of the youth brought to stand before him. During the circumcision, the elders, collapsing around each youth as he was brought before *nyamero,* shouted, "Don't be afraid," and "If you run, they'll kill you." The older initiates were told to put their hands above their heads, to be brave and not cry out. The younger were often held fast as they kicked and screamed and tried to get away.

Meeting the heron in the bush is perceived as an ordeal. There is a secret word, *emungen,* which refers to the suffering of pain, heat, faintness, and blood loss of Kombutsu. Some individuals are "caught" by *emungen* more intensively than others. *Emungen* can be worse if a father hovers near his son while the cutting takes place, or if a participant broke certain food taboos or drank too much wine the day before Kombutsu. A youth who fainted from *emungen* was awakened by a rifle shot close to his ear. I was also told, but did not myself see, that metal bracelets are sometimes placed in initiates' mouths to prevent them from biting their tongues. Sometimes initiates defecate out of fear, and are later teased with great irony: "During Kombutsu, he took down the heron." Ehing say that the loud singing of the visitors serves to drown out any cries from the bush which might reach the ears of women in the village. Inside the bush, the songs and strutting and waving of sticks and guns heightened the passion of all who were within.

As each youth was cut, he was led deeper into the bush until he reached another small clearing where, with other initiates of his lineage, he sat on a small termite hill. Each youth was immediately given two sticks to clap together. Elders also brought small twigs which they placed under the penis of each initiate to prop it up. The twigs were held in place with cord wrapped around the youth's thighs. I was told that the twig served to hold the penis straight, lest it heal crooked. In one village, Bafikan, the twig was called *nyamero,* for the fork is said to resemble the heron's crest. As the initiates sat and clapped, they were visited by elders and strangers who sang and danced and offered words of encouragement. Some elders sympathetically clapped for youth too dazed to do so themselves, and others offered explanations of why they had bled more then their friends: "You must have drunk too much yesterday." But along with the words of sympathy, there were taunts as well, offered mainly by the visitors. In their rounds inspecting the youth, they would sometimes say, "Your sex hurts?!" and "Who cut your sex?!"

The elders also peered at the cuts to make sure the job had been well done. A good cutting would provoke a compliment, but in a few cases, the "heron" was called back to better complete his work. When all the cutting had been finished, the "herons" were given wine to wash their knives and their hands. Some people came up to me and said, "Kombutsu is finished," by which they referred not only to the cutting but to the fact that now I had seen the most important and secret aspect of the ritual.

For an hour or so nothing else happened apart from the constant visitations and inspections of one group of initiates and then another. By late afternoon, the hosts brought out to the bush the wine collected before the ritual. All drank save the initiates themselves. About an hour later, the initiates were given leaves to wrap around their wounds and shortly thereafter they were led out of the bush to begin the march toward the Kahus spirit. The march was slow and punctuated with short dances and gunfire. Several of the younger children were carried, and I saw one initiate carrying a gourd to catch the drops of blood which were still falling.

As the villagers approached the clearing of Kahus, the procession stopped and the initiates were given a chance to urinate before entering the area. Then they went into the clearing and the initiates saw the huts where they were to live. Elders of each House served their children an evening meal called *buna:* the rice of *buna* was given by the youth's mother's brothers in May and then each mother contributed it to the House meal on the day of Kombutsu. After the meal, fathers laid out mats in the huts, lit fires, and everyone went to sleep.

The next day, the very youngest children in the village were circumcised. They did not participate on the first day because of the special difficulties of handling and watching over them amid so much commotion. They too witnessed a libation on their behalf at the House's Kahin, but they did not walk out into the rice fields. Instead, they went directly to Kahus. There, just before entering the clearing, they were cut. After this work, the cutters took their formal leave. They gave a speech at the Kahus, wishing the initiates peace and a quick recovery. For their efforts, they had been paid with a meal and wine or with money. A Bakunum elder joined in the speeches, telling the youth not to cover their sex with their cloths, so that the wind might enter and cool their wounds.

In the next two weeks, other latecomers entered Kombutsu. These persons were either those in the army who could not take leave in time for the ritual, or a few who had been delayed by national examinations in the University. For these, an Ehing from another village came to do the cutting. He was also asked to recut a few of the youngest children whose original wounds had been slight. For though the intent of Kombutsu is to remove the foreskin, the cutters were less severe with the very small boys. The major idea of the ritual is to spill sexual blood, and with the very young just the tip of the skin is considered sufficient for them to have entered the initiation. However, the wounds on some children had closed up, "as if the child had not been cut," and needed to be reopened. The second cutting was much more extensive.

Closing the Initiation

Two weeks after opening the ritual, Bakunum "blocked up the path" of the initiation. This is the act which "closes Kombutsu," and after which there can be no more cutting. According to tradition, Bakunum was a week late in doing so, and other villages that had not waited for tardy participants had closed the ritual a week before.

To "block up the path," the initiates were escorted during the night to the meander where they washed themselves for the first time. Before jumping into the water, the youth removed the leaves which had covered their wounds since the circumcision and gave these to an elder. Then in they went, shouting about the initial sting of the salty water but enjoying themselves just the same. The people say that the water is good for the wounds, and one father even carried some of it back to the Kahus so that he could dress his son's wound periodically. As the initiates played in the water, the elders chewed a bitter and oily plant called *ishiare* which is believed to promote healing. They spit out the mashed leaves on the youth as they emerged from the water. The group then walked back toward the village, singing songs. Apa Seba carefully carried the leaf bandages and later stored these in a leaf container at the Kahus.

Back in the village, Bunesi, the elder responsible for Kahus, gave the following speech:

> There, we have washed the children. The week we should have closed the path, we let it pass because the children hadn't come. The Ehing went ahead of us. God pardon us, may all the children be healed, so that we exit together as we entered together. We don't say that someone who enters last will be the last to be healed. We go libate at the Kahus, that the spirit comes in the night to lick the sex of the children. A child who has vision, he must help heal his friend and not use the force to increase the pain. The spirit doesn't like someone to do that. Each belongs to the spirit. God must cover if someone ate his friend. We said a person will not be lost here. A person [who is dead] must miss his friend [who may be a witch]; when we exit, he will then go struggle there.

A word of explanation. In the speech, the elder alludes to Kahus as the guardian of the children, as the spirit that will lick their wounds. He also admonishes any children who have vision, which is a power to do good or bad, to only do good; in a later speech, he added that those with vision should not give others bad dreams. That which God must "cover" is witchcraft. As we have seen, an individual who has been killed will seek revenge; the elder was asking the victim to delay his retribution until after the initiation. Kombutsu was now closed.

Life at the Kahus

Perhaps the signal event of the initiation, apart from the actual circumcision, occurred directly after the initiates moved from bush to Kahus. As they arrived, the youth were told, informally and by whomever was at hand, how human reproduction occurs. Just as, when giving birth, a woman is told that during the male initiation it is not *nyamero* (the heron) who arrives, but a stranger who cuts the men's sex, the initiates learn what occurs in childbirth during their Kombutsu. I heard the following statements:

> As you bleed now, the sex of a woman bleeds when she gives birth. . . . A woman spreads her legs, they are held open with a cooking stick, and a cloth is laid out to catch the child. . . . A woman may lick the child; the child is given water to drink to see if it is a person. . . . Sometimes a cloth is put in her mouth to stifle her cries. . . . At birth, her clitoris is cut. It's their Kombutsu. . . . The clitoris is cut three times, for the first three births. This makes the child come out more easily. . . . A child comes out of her sex. . . . When a woman's sitting is bad, blood is coming out of her sex. She takes a cloth and pulls it tightly against her. . . . Now you can sleep with women more easily.

As elders themselves have not seen a birth and as no attempt is made to arrive at a common understanding of the experience, what they pass on is by no means a uniform account. To the best of my knowledge, no stick is used to aid a birth; nor do Ehing practice any form of clitorectomy. It may be that, as men see their Kombutsu as similar to the experience of women, they assume that women also cut.

Apart from this information about birth, the initiates also learned in the days that followed the songs of Kombutsu which are only sung by elders and only in the forest. The youth first heard these in the rice fields, but most were too dazed to pay them much attention. Furthermore, almost none of these are in the Ehing language but in a Diola dialect or a language of Guinea-Bissau. I was not allowed to record the actual singing, but these are some of the songs as they were translated to me.

Emungen w-o-o-o-o-
sali salio o-i-i.
[*emungen* is the suffering when cut;
sali is the ridge of the penis.
As in all the songs,
much of the melody is carried by sounds that are not words.]

w-o-o-o *asunguru*.
She goes to give birth like a goat.
Who said that?
Emungen o-o-o-o.
[*asunguru* means girl.]

w-o-o-o-i w-o-o-a.
Don't fear *amanyen*.
It's natural to have a sex.
The small knife has already cut.
[*amanyen* is a priest, here the head of Odieng.]

The vagina is narrow o-o-i-i-i.
It is sweet.
[though it was thought narrow. . . .]

W-o-o-i-i Djamuaa [a man's name] had blocked Kahus.
Emungen w-o-o-o-i-i
SAS.
[SAS is onomatopoeia for the sound of a cutting knife.
Before *emungen,* before being cut,
no one could enter Kahus.]

O-i-i-e-e-w-o-o-i.
The vagina has a long mouth.
If you look there are teeth.
The penis enters o-w-e-e-i-i-SAS.

W-o-o-o. Anare had a big vagina.
W-o-o-h-e-e-i.
When she urinates, out comes a child.

W-o-o-o-e-e w-o-o-e.
A great village sang a Kombutsu.
Ambia [the priest], Why did he do that?
W-o-o the rich man!

The initiates sang these songs and danced before each meal. Two
elders played the drums that were positioned at the center of the clearing,

and the youth circled around them as they chanted. The youth also sang and danced in response to the "master of the forest." The voice first beckoned them the very night of Kombutsu—several hours after the initiates had bedded down. With the noise, they were exhorted to rise and dance and did so, until Bunesi, the elder who serves the spirit, pounded on the fence surrounding the shrine and said, "Hey, hey, hey pardon them, they fear." And with that request, the "master" became quiet and the youth went back to sleep. During the remaining nights in the forest, the "master" often would demand dancing. Sometimes, when the initiates had danced well during the day, they were awakened only once, but sometimes the "master" would voice its demands three or more times and the youth would get little sleep.

The "master" also made tours of the village at night. As it approached a house, those within whispered that the "elder" was coming and closed their doors and dimmed their lamps. In passing, it sometimes toppled mortars and other objects in a courtyard. I was told that when the "master" turned over the mortar in a particular courtyard in 1953, its act signaled that a woman living there was a witch and warned her not to harm the initiates. The death of any woman the year after Kombutsu is likely to be attributed to her witchcraft or to the belief that she had come in the night to look into the Kahus area.

The initiates themselves never knew the source of the sound, for when men played the instrument they always stood behind the fence surrounding the spirit. According to tradition, those who played should have been naked, but the individuals I observed were always clothed. Not everyone dared spin the "master," for its power was said to be forceful enough to pull people along with it until they fell; but middle-aged men as well as old men played it, and there were no restrictions attached to doing so.

During their stay in the forest, the initiates were subject to various proscriptions. Most emphatically, they were not allowed to go "up high"—that is, they could not sit on logs or stools, or climb trees. The termite hills on which they sat after being cut are thought an extension of the ground. They also were not allowed, according to tradition, to wash their hands until their wounds were completely healed, though in this Kombutsu the initiates began to wash after their initial visit to the meander. But they did not bathe, and their only clothing remained the striped cloth, which also could not be washed. The initiates were dirty, and perhaps ritually as well as literally, although no explicit statement was made about their moral condition. Elders eschewed certain forms of contact with them. In the first several weeks, the youth were required to greet visitors by offering their sticks rather than hands, and they were not allowed to touch either the water pots or the drinking cups. Instead, elders held the cups for them. On the other hand, such forms of contact as touching an initiate or treating his wound were not restricted.

Near the end of the seclusion period, some of these proscriptions were not as stringently enforced. Even though initiates should never sit on logs during the whole of the seclusion, some eventually did so, which did not disquiet the elders. The restrictions on their behavior were thought to promote healing; therefore, they were relaxed somewhat when the more ostensible dangers had passed. In the beginning, however, the initiates were carefully watched, for great opprobrium is attached to a child who dies in the forest. I was told that a cord would be attached to his neck and that he would be dragged naked around the Kahus area. He would be buried without clothes in the bush and with sticks placed through his body so that his soul would not rise as a zombie. A child is believed to die during Kombutsu either because he has committed a taboo of Odieng and has not confessed, or because he is a witch, and in the context of Kombutsu these reasons are not clearly disassociated.

No one died during this initiation. Certainly the fact that many fathers had bought antibiotics helped keep down the incidence of infection, and some even had had their children vaccinated against tetanus. Still, there were moments of real concern. One night I was called over by a friend to look at a four-year-old who, for no apparent reason, had discharged blood from his penis "as if he had just been cut." The blood, however, came from within and not from the wound. At the time there was nothing we could do, and the child was better the next day. The initiates also once developed a bad cough, which made its way throughout the camp. The fathers contributed money and sent someone to Ziguinchor to buy medicine; they also held a public meeting to discuss the illness. During the meeting, one of the younger fathers dramatically challenged the oldest men and, through them, the Kahus spirit itself. Why, he questioned, if we asked Kahus to keep the children well, are they now sick? If the sickness continues, "the Kahus is something without anything!" As he later explained to me, he was trying to shame the spirit and elders into doing their work.

Compared with the hazing that is often a central element in initiations elsewhere, I found fathers solicitous rather than authoritative. Even when they invoked their authority, I gained the impression that, as we might say, they only did so for the children's good. To do things by tradition was to serve the spirits and thereby obligate them to guard and keep the children. And so, when elders yelled that the children should dance more enthusiastically, or learn the songs, or play the drum ("If you don't learn, who will play at funerals for your generation?"), they did so in order that

Kombutsu would end in *mazunemi,* in peace and well-being. And when they yelled, the initiates would often respond: "Excuse us, and don't be angry. If we do *munyo,* correct us, because we don't know anything." Still, there was one night when the elders seemed particularly heavy-handed. The youth refused to rise and dance in the middle of the night. They complained that they were tired and that, when they danced, their wounds became painful. The elders then mocked the youth, saying, "But you manage to dance all night with your girl friends." They were refer-ring to the dances the youth hold in their hall during the rainy season, dances complete with a battery-operated stereo. They continued, "You said you wanted to wrestle *nyamero;* well, *nyamero* was stronger!" Then, more threateningly, they added that Kombutsu was not over, that the next phase was to take a heated wire and push it into the mouth of the initiates' penises. When the youth countered that they would flee, the elders as-sured them that they would be caught. The youth danced, and the "mas-ter" was appeased.

The initiates were to stay in the bush until all their wounds were healed, for otherwise women might know through a public disclosure what Kombutsu is all about. The daily round was oriented around the three meals. For each, the rice was cooked in the village by the unmarried women of each House and then carried by young girls to a spot about a hundred yards from Kahus. These girls also drew and transported water to the same point. Both rice and water were then taken to the Kahus area by "carriers," teenage youth from other societies who had already been initiated. Some of these youth came from Guinea-Bissau and some from Diola groups. Any rice left over from a meal was thrown away, for it could not be returned to the village or be saved to be eaten the following day. Each House initially served the rice which had been collected before Kombutsu, and, when this stock ran low, the fathers again made mea-sured contributions.

During the first days after their entrance, the initiates did little but eat, sleep, and dance, but, as they began to feel better, their activities became more varied. They began to play quiet games with sticks and boards drawn in the sand, and they started to wander a little outside the Kahus clearing. But there was little to do, and soon the youngest children were running, jumping, and even wrestling. Some reopened their cuts, and fathers did their best to keep them under control. To break the monotony, the initiates on July 11 asked permission to go fishing at the meander. Fish is considered more acceptable food than meat, whose grease is thought to delay healing. The elders granted their request and arranged the first of several excursions. The youth left the Kahus area before dawn and did not return until after dusk; when they went, the women in the village were warned to stay away. About this time also, fathers, who at first hardly left the area, began to absent themselves from the Kahus to plant their nurseries. Because of the ritual, seeding had been seriously delayed.

Leaving the Forest

As the weeks went by, the elders' concerns became increasingly oriented toward the question, when would the initiates leave the forest? Would all the children of Bakunum be healed when other villages called for the termination of Kombutsu? Some of the youngest children had been well since mid-July, though they kept their bandages on to hide their good fortune, perhaps because they were wary of the "jealousy" of their peers. But many of the wounds, especially those of the older initiates, lingered. On July 22, the elders again asked for the aid of Kahus.

> Bakunum be quiet. We are here today for the children whom we have led from the hands of their mothers. We've come to keep them here. We ask that God lick them and heal them. If God gave any individual force, when he goes he will cringe down [and not disturb others, or cause them bad dreams], and when he returns, he will let his friends sleep. Ehing are saying that the hour has come. God pardon us, so that the children heal quickly. It would be shameful, if Ehing were to call, and we only ask, how now? For us, there remain some [persons still not healed]. The day we leave, if a child were to leave with his sore, how would we speak to his mother? That's what is *munyo* for Ehing.

In this speech, the elder again raised the problem of keeping knowledge of Kombutsu from women, and, in view of traditional practice, his phrasing is euphemistic. I was told that in former times it was forbidden to exit while still wounded, and therefore an unwell initiate would be killed and buried without public announcement. In 1953 some did leave the forest unwell; they were not killed at that time because of fear of government reprisal. But for that privilege, the initiates were assessed the fine of one bull which they killed at the Kahus in 1979. They were also cut on the leg when leaving the forest to provide a public excuse why they could not join in the dancing at the end of the ritual.

Four days after this speech at Bakunum, the villagers of Kalian braved an inspection of their initiates. Bakunum followed the next day. The youth were told to line up and remove their bandages. The elders found that only eleven were still not ready to leave the bush. They told the youth to seek leaves to cure their wounds, but this advice was generally ignored. Instead, the youth used Western medicines.

Shortly thereafter, Sisa arrived at Bakunum; then he walked to the other villages to hear the results of their inspections. As head of Odieng, he was the first to make a judgment about when to end the ritual. With his assessment made, Sisa went to see Abiton Bassene, an elder who lived in the village of Dialang. Abiton is responsible for calling any meeting of the population, religious or secular, which is to be held in a large clearing on his House's land. According to tradition, the men meet in that clearing to discuss and set the date for ending Kombutsu. Sisa gave Abiton the signal to call the meeting.

On July 31 we heard that Abiton had set the meeting for August 8. Because the end, like the entrance, of the initiation must fall on the week-day *ozalum* and because there were a number of stages leading to the termination, Abiton's decision meant that the earliest possible date for leaving the forest was August 21. Abiton's decision provoked an immediate and angry reaction in Bakunum. It was already late in the season, and many felt that it was past time to end Kombutsu and get on with the agricultural work. Indeed, some of the initiates had families to feed and could not even work their fields sporadically as could the older members of the population. Back in June, some men had predicted to me that because of the rice they would be out of the forest by August 1.

That afternoon, some individuals went to discuss the problem with Sisa and others went to elicit the reaction in other villages. Their major argument was that by August 15 the women should have already begun their transplanting—waiting any longer would forfeit precious days of rain. Sisa agreed to go early the next morning to Dialang, and he was met on the path by Mossi.

They presented the implications of his decision to Abiton. But he initially refused to change the date. He capitulated only when he was told that the responsibility for the ruin of rice would rest on his head. Abiton agreed to move up the meeting two days, which theoretically would allow an exit on the 15th.

But mid-morning the next day we heard that Abiton had reneged and spread the word that the date of the meeting was "fixed." It was to be the 8th, as he originally had announced. Hearing the news, the elders were livid. Together they raged about the reasons for Abiton's uncompromising attitude: that, with no children, he slept at home and not in the damp woods and, besides, he was jealous of others as well; that he did not need to contribute rice to the meals at Kahus and was thinking "only of his stomach," of the free goods he was enjoying; and that his village, Dialang, against the rules, had cut some tardy arrivals after Kombutsu had been closed, and Abiton was delaying the exit so that they would have time to heal. In a rebuke to Abiton, many Ehing decided to meet on the 5th anyway. No one from Dialang attended, and neither did some of the middle-aged men from other villages who had been most vocal about an early termination. I never fully understood why some of these did not come to that meeting. With their absence and out of a sense of inertia, the date stood. When it comes to dealing with spirits, Ehing tend to be conservative. No one dared to take on the possibility of crossing a power when one would be responsible for the consequences.

On the 8th, Dialang went to the clearing for the originally scheduled meeting, and this time no one from the other villages attended. Abiton then sent word that there was to be another meeting the 11th. That day was an airing of disagreements. Abiton began by stating, with a postured naiveté, that he had heard the Ehing assembled on the 5th but did not know why. There followed accusation and counter-accusation, threats to leave Kombutsu immediately, and taunts that Dialang could wait and wait until there would be nothing but famine the next year. With the date now fixed for the 21st, however, the group decided that on the 15th each village would hold a preliminary ritual called "Accompanying On the Path," and then dispersed.

"Accompanying On the Path" is essentially a dance, the purpose of which is to display the initiates before their mothers who, until this time, had been uncertain whether they were alive or dead. Throughout the initiation, a mother had not referred to her child by his name. Instead, when meeting her husband, she would ask, "My monkey, is he there?" To which a father would always reply, "Yes" and would have done so even if the initiate had died.

On August 15, then, all the women of the village came to a clearing just outside of the Kahus area. One by one each initiate was accompanied by an elder to a position in front of the women where the youth would dance for a minute (Fig. 5.1) and then be led away. When a mother saw her son, or when a sister saw her brother, she would dance with joy and sometimes throw gifts. Most women threw rice or mangoes, but one girl threw a bottle of soda pop. But there was still no close contact between males and females, for a makeshift fence had been constructed between the dancing initiates and the women.

Immediately after this display, which lasted about an hour, each initiate chose a girl of the village with whom he would exchange wine for her rice after Kombutsu. The initiates' choices were communicated by elders, and fathers chose girls for their very young sons. After Kombutsu, the girl would send the initiate a meal of fish and rice, and later during the

Fig. 5.1. Initiates emerge from the seclusion of Kombutsu to dance before the women of the village, who are relieved to see the youth and greet them with joy.

dry season the initiate would give her a gift of some 20 liters of wine. I was told that this prestation was enough, should both parties consent, to give the initiate rights to marry the woman. If the chosen girl, on the other hand, had the same patronym as the initiate, this prestation might mark the start of a fictive brother–sister relationship.

The dance of "Accompanying On the Path" by definition tempered the separation of the sexes that had been in force during Kombutsu, for now women could see the initiates. But their relations were still not normal. The initiates still did not go near the residential areas in the village and were not allowed to speak to women. The complete return to everyday life did not occur until after the initiates visited Odieng.

Both the comments and the sighs of tired elders and initiates indicated that, for most, the day of departure came none too soon. For close to two months they had been sleeping out in the rain and nursing various fevers and coughs. On the morning of the final day, the initiates again were shaved, and in the afternoon they were led out of the Kahus area into the woods, so that the elders were left alone at the Kahus shrine to make final ritual preparations. An old man brought out the bloodied leaves which had been stored after the first visit to the meander, and these were burned into an ash. With the ashes in hand, the elders entered the inner fence surrounding the Kahus for a final libation. For this libation, each House in the village contributed one gourd of wine. And after the libation, the "master of the forest" was buried at the Kahus. I was told that traditionally the "master" was buried wrapped in the cloth of one of the initiates, though this was not done in 1979. The elders then poured the ash from the leaves into the libation pitcher, where it was mixed with wine and taken from behind the fence.

The initiates were then gathered together and led to a pond in the rice fields. One by one they went to the pond, took in a mouthful of water, spit out the water to their left and right, and then dunked their heads. Afterward, they returned to the Kahus. Here, again one by one, they approached an elder who held the container of wine mixed with the ash of the bloodied leaves. Each initiate fell to his knees and drank some of the wine but did not touch the container with his hands.

Elders then addressed the children for the last time at the Kahus. At Bakunum the initiates heard five speeches, several of which reiterated similar points. One elder began his speech saying, "You have drunk poison" (the wine and ash) and then went on to say that the initiates were leaving the bush in *mazunemi,* that no one had died as even witches had been protected at Kahus. Furthermore, all the "hands," that is, curses, of the other spirits had been lifted during Kombutsu. But now Kahus would no longer afford protection, and past victims of witchcraft might seek revenge "at home." With this warning other elders went on to exhort the initiates not to be "jealous" of each other and to "let others grow up." Everyone had equally spent his rice during Kombutsu, they said, and so to be short of rice was no cause for jealousy. And rather than be jealous of the productive work of others and attempt to ruin it, they were to remember that the well-off should lend to those in need.

The elders also spoke of the initiates' new status as elders (*abia*) and of the taboos which they learned. Even with this knowledge, they were told, it is still *munyo,* and more so, to "go to the side of women." "Don't look at the cloths of menstruating women, and don't look for the blood where they have sat." Though women know the Kombutsu songs, the initiates were reminded it is forbidden to sing those in their presence. They were told to keep all their new knowledge in their heads, to keep the taboos of their fathers, and to go to Odieng if they should see something by accident.

The speeches finished, fathers went home to fetch new clothing for the initiates, who wandered about until dusk. At that time they shed their ragged striped cloths, handed these to the elders in charge of Kahus, and walked out of the Kahus area to put on new indigo cloths and red hats. Unmarried initiates put a string of beads around their wrists; those married put them around their necks. Some of the old cloths were distributed among the old men of the village. Bunesi, the elder of Kahus, kept those which remained. Any women unable to conceive or faced with the deaths of many children may buy or wear the cloths to correct their difficulties.

The initiates and elders left Kahus as the sun set, and the entrances to the area were blocked. Eventually everything there would be burned. The procession, initiates holding their decorated circumcision sticks high, went to the residential areas in the village and bedded down on the verandas of the houses. Traditionally, they stayed in the bush adjacent to the houses, but they slept this year on the verandas in deference to the rain. Late into the night the women in the houses were singing, dancing, and drinking.

The Visit to Odieng

For most Ehing, the most intense and meaningful moment of Kombutsu had been the circumcision itself. I remember explaining that, for my part, I was also interested in the initiates' visit to Odieng, and I remember as well that my friends could not imagine that I did not find the cutting itself, which they guard so secretly, much the more important event. But I was trying to fit Kombutsu into their system of thought. I must have seemed doubly odd when I insisted on attending the very first performances at Odieng, rituals that were necessary for the return of youth to village life. Sisa had informed me that the initiates would begin to visit the spirit "right after the first crow of the rooster." The same ritual, my friends suggested, would be repeated throughout the day as all of the Houses in turn brought their youth to the shrine. Why go to Nyame before dawn? My reasoning was simple, if a bit obsessive. I was afraid that after a few performances the elders, out of boredom or fatigue, would begin to abridge the rite, and I had not waited about all summer to see that.

Mossi agreed to escort me to Sisa's village, and we set out together after a few hours of sleep. But after perhaps a hundred yards, he asked me if I knew the way, and he returned home to bed. I walked on, and just as I was leaving the territory of Bakunum, it started to rain. At first there were only a few drops, but then the monsoon came rolling in from the east. Next, my flashlight began to fade. Within minutes of walking along the forest paths, I had become completely lost. I doubled back but could not pick up the trail; all four paths looked like the one I had come from. I stood there for a while, trying to spot a landmark during the flashes of lightning. But the bush—recently cut and burnt for rice nurseries—now looked unfamiliar. At one point I squatted down to pull my poncho over my sneakers while I tried to figure out what to do. I even tried yelling for help, but no Ehing would come out in the middle of a rainy night to meet some screaming zombie (*nyazango*).

There was nothing to do but go forward, though I feared both that I would wander far and that the ritual had already begun. But I finally saw a fence of fronds and knew that I was either near a manioc field out in the forest or near a house. The fence indeed led to a house, and I saw some initiates sleeping on the front porch. I still had no idea where I was. The house, it turned out, was Sisa's. The activities, to my surprise and my relief, had not yet progressed beyond sleeping.

I sat on the porch for an hour or so, now impatient, and finally I heard elders stirring. It was about dawn—the roosters were on their second or third round—when we all straggled out back to Odieng's shrine. There Sisa began the ritual, and the two lineages which comprise his village made their confessions. While these were taking place, a lineage from Bafikan and one from a small village called Kuguo arrived, lineages which, according to tradition, are the next to participate.

When the elders from these villages had settled down, a dispute broke out about the form of the rite. One old man questioned Sisa's direction, specifically the order of two consecutive acts. In his view, they should have been reversed. Sisa began to question the procedure with his old friend. Listening to the elders argue over their memories of a ritual twenty-five years distant, I began to feel the irony of my midnight trek—of my plan to see the perfect performance of this ritual. I was watching the elders as I had come to know them, independent and defiant to the last. What happened next compounded the irony of my situation. Sisa nodded in my direction. Called on for my opinion, I joined the others in a style of debate I had so often observed in silence; and my view that Sisa was right, and that was that, was received quite naturally, as if I were as able as anyone else to voice a point of view. A minor contribution to a long summer; Sisa grunted affirmatively, and the ritual continued.

All during Kombutsu, Odieng had been closed to any confession for a breach of its rules and did not open again until after receiving the initiates. Like the ritual for widows, the visit for the initiates differed from the ritual I first described in Chapter 3. Most conspicuously, this is a group ritual in which all the youth of a House are gathered on the steps of the shrine and drink the blood of a single rooster. As the initiates approached, one held a gourd of wine on his head and carried the rooster in his hand. These were handed to Sisa, and all the youth sat down with their backs to him. Sisa put the empty libation pitcher on the head of the youth farthest to his left, and an elder of the House, sitting off to the side, spoke for the initiates. The speeches of all these elders were remarkably similar throughout the day.

Mani [a greeting given to spirits]—You see the children have come today to finish, for we have washed them. As they entered the forest, some went up high. When you perform the ritual today, we libate so the children will enter the house in *mazunemi*.

Sisa then moved the pitcher to the head of the next child and so on down the row, as the elder repeated his speech for each.

The rooster was killed, and the mixture of blood and wine was given to each initiate to drink. Sisa spit pure wine on the back of the first initiate, placed his hands on his shoulders, and then, bending close to the youth's ear, softly spoke (Fig. 5.2). Unlike the ritual for transgressors, Sisa did not repeat the confession. Instead, he greeted the past priests of the spirit:

> *Amanya man* [greetings to the priest] *Niham* [*kaham*—to greet] *Kutilumo, niham Obolega, niham Obunyame, niham Okumbulan, niham Oneedora, niham Obelega, niham Obuovone, niham Ota, Kapuwa nihame.*

As Sisa made this greeting, Samaila, at the head of the shrine, poured out wine. Sisa spoke in each initiate's ear in turn, then blew in their ears, and sent them home.

That day, I left Ehingland. I was disappointed not to be able to stay for the celebration—a week of dances, good meals, and visits—but I was expected to begin teaching within the week. By the time I had packed, the last persons were leaving Odieng's shrine, and some friends then helped me carry my things to the road.

The Final Rite

Though the youth (*ahula*) were now elders (*abia*), they still did not know about the "master of the forest." They were to learn what made this sound several months later, in December, at a ceremony called Bunoken (from *kanoken*, "to be dirty"), but these initiates would not actually see the "master" until it was again made for the next Kombutsu. At Bunoken, I was told, the initiates gather at the grand Odieng for the first time, where a bull is sacrificed and they drink a mixture of its blood and wine. A second sacrifice takes place later at Kahus. It is only after Bunoken that they can go see the initiation of others.

An Interpretation of Kombutsu: The Definition of Sexual Powers

I have presented a lengthy account of Kombutsu because, let me repeat, it is the most important of Ehing rituals. Now our problem is to understand

Fig. 5.2. Odieng at the end of Kombutsu. The shrine is located in the center of the small hut.

why Ehing find its performance so essential. To do so is also to understand the various rules of Odieng that focus on this event.

Kombutsu, Ehing will say explicitly, is the male counterpart of birth. Physically, the two events are similar in that in both individuals bleed from their sexual organs. They are also a counterpart in a jural sense in that both events are transitions during which youth (*ahula*) become elders (*abia*). With these moments of passage, the taboos of foreknowledge are lifted by definition, males and females learn how their opposite bleeds, and all thereafter may see the dead. In addition, initiates may now eat two foods, eggs and a nut called *tio,* which hitherto were forbidden. Had *ahula* eaten these foods before the initiation, Ehing say they would have bled excessively.

The initiation is a complex ritual and certainly one that is susceptible to varying interpretations. Perhaps the most direct and fundamental question to ask, however, is why men cut themselves. Since Ehing think of Kombutsu as the counterpart of birth, the answer is patent. Men cut themselves in initiation to bleed as women bleed in birth. The identification of the two events is the reason that men project that, as they cut themselves, women also use a knife in the process of birth. Though it may be too literal an interpretation to claim that during Kombutsu men "give birth" (and I would not do so), the spilling of blood represents, at the least, their sexuality. Kombutsu can be seen as the dramatization of men's procreative capacities, of their powers of generation. For this reason, the ragged cloths worn by the initiates can make women fertile and can prevent miscarriages. Also for this reason, the initiates choose prospective partners near the end of the ritual, and the elders, in their final speeches, urge the initiates toward marriage.

That Kombutsu is a celebration of sexuality is an interpretation that helps account for and explain the initiates' visit to Odieng. Rituals at Odieng concern contact between social categories, and this instance is no different. Here the initiates themselves are not caught by the spirit—but they would be if they resumed normal relations with women before the visit to the shrine. What, then, is the source of their ambiguity? I can only conclude that it derives from the idea that men are bleeding, through a ritual act, as women (naturally) bleed in birth. The point to make here is not that men covet women's reproductive power but that they borrow a sign of it to express their own. It makes sense that, as men borrow a sign of feminine power, Odieng keeps women themselves away from the event.

It is because the symbolic equivalence between initiation and birth is unidirectional—it is men who bleed like women rather than women who bleed like men—that men must visit Odieng after Kombutsu, but women need not visit the shrine after birth. The spatial idioms of the two events are reversed, but this reversal shows their inner connection. We have seen that women must give birth in men's houses. Men, on the other hand, must shed blood out of their houses and cannot reenter them until they are no longer acting as the counterpart of women but, instead, are acting as their normal selves.

The notion that the bleeding of men is a sign modeled on feminine power is made clear during the confession at Odieng. Each elder who spoke on behalf of the initiates referred essentially only to the taboo of going "up high." When I asked why, if this taboo might only have been broken by a few, the confession was made for all, Ehing replied that some of the others might have forgotten what they did. Certainly, this is a response to my query rather than a serious explanation. For there is in principle no specific transgression to remember: rather, the confession about going "up high" refers to the state of having bled, and this characterizes the condition of all the participants. Consequently, having borrowed a sign of female sexuality, the initiates must then ingest rooster blood to displace this association; thereafter, as men, they may come into contact with women.

Sisa's response to the confession in the ritual is more difficult to analyze. In the form of the ritual when an individual has been caught by Odieng, Sisa sometimes repeats the gist of the confession but always exhorts Odieng to "let go" of the sick individual. After the initiation, this did not occur. Instead, Sisa greeted the elders of the shrine who had preceded him as the spirit received its gift. As he almost whispered the names of the elders in the initiates' ears, it looked very much like an introduction, as if the initiates were meeting those who represent a vital area of Ehing tradition. As these elders represent the work of the spirit, the initiates, having realized their generative capacities as men, came face to face with what governs the order of their society.

In this regard, there is a telling connection between what the cutting in Kombutsu represents and the rules that organize the ritual. I have stated that an initiate must shed blood in the same village as his father, but in a later Kombutsu. These rules—that the ritualized sexuality of fathers must precede that of sons, and especially that this progression must be associated with a particular locality—evoke the idea of a cycle of souls. It seems that the rules root male sexuality to land. In more formal terms, the rules that organize Kombutsu suggest that this ritual not only represents male sexuality but also a principle of descent. This is the major message of the event.

The Problem of Knowledge

There are two modes of knowledge associated with Kombutsu: that concerning the Kombutsu of the opposite sex and that concerning fore-knowledge. The essential point about sexual knowledge is that it not be given public expression. If women already know what occurs during Kombutsu, why try to deceive them by cutting an unhealed youth's leg? Why wait so long before leaving the bush? Simply because mystery is used to make a social statement about separation, about the meaning of categories, about the autonomy of sexual capacities. It is almost beside the point to ask, what do the women really know? It would make little difference if they knew everything—as long as they kept it, as Ehing might say, in their heads.

Similarly, Odieng's rule about foreknowledge serves to differentiate categories—elders and youth. In today's climate, in an age of high school students and extensive travel, this rule is often compromised. When I first arrived among the people in 1975, the youth who knew French had translated Kombutsu for me as *la circoncision*. The elders, too, clearly realized that the veil of secrecy was no longer effective. When libating at the grand Odieng in May, Sisa, I was told, prayed that those who already "knew about *nyamero* (the heron)" should forget their knowledge until the moment they stood in front of him. But the problem was even more

graphic: some students arrived for Kombutsu already cut. Lest they suffer
the consequences of a bad cutting or infection, they had had themselves
circumcised in hospitals. The elders in each village then had to decide if
these youth should be allowed to "enter Kombutsu." Permission was
granted. When these youth entered the bush, they were cut on their
thighs. At least *nyamero* drew some blood.

Again, the issue concerns the public expression of knowledge. But
the elders also often attributed the taboos on foreknowledge to the practical function of limiting anxiety about birth and Kombutsu. They thought
that initiates might be more reluctant to enter the forest if they knew what
lay ahead. Ehing perceive both initiation and childbirth as ordeals, fraught
with dangers and the possibility of death. Like women who are thought to
hover between life and death during childbirth, initiates are considered at
risk. During initiation mothers were unsure whether their children would
live or die, and male elders admonished youths that it was taboo to die in
the forest.

The most palpable danger in these events is excessive loss of blood.
The power of *emungen*—the seizure of faintness and heat when meeting
the heron—finds in bleeding its empirical correlative. Once cut, the
initiates, like bleeding women, are forbidden to go "up high." Should
they do so, they would be caught by Odieng. Odieng will also catch a
youth if he has broken any of its rules and not yet confessed them—and
will catch the youth while he remains in the forest. Even if a youth had
committed his act years before, Odieng is said often to wait for Kombutsu
before attacking. Thus again, as we found in the instance of menstruation,
there is a precise correspondence between an intrinsic feature of an event
(initiates bleeding) and the form of affliction brought on by the spirit.

In this connection, it can be seen that the *munyo* of Odieng are a means
to control the experience of Kombutsu (and childbirth), for to observe the
taboos implies the avoidance of that which could be so much the worse.
Franz Steiner (1956: 147) has described how prohibitions narrow down
and define dangerous situations:

> Taboo gives notice that danger lies not in the whole situation, but
> only in certain specified actions concerning it. These actions, these
> danger spots, are more challenging and more deadly than the danger
> of the situation as a whole, for the whole situation can be rendered
> free from danger by dealing with it, or, rather, avoiding the specified
> danger spots completely.

So Odieng, by promising an intensification of danger, in effect tempers
these events.

The Cultural Control of Blood

There is yet another way the people seem to use ritual to modify the experience of blood loss. I refer here to the ash of the bloodied leaves the initiates drink and to the bull's blood ingested several months later at the grand Odieng and at Kahus.

Why the ash? One elder told me that it is the ash which gives Kombutsu its "value"; another said, "If you don't drink, your vision (face) will be clouded." The notion of "unclear vision" is often used by Ehing to describe states of moral and physical distress; hence, it is not a specific explanation. For example, having "unclear vision" may be used to characterize a soul which cannot find out why it died, a person who is caught by the power of *emungen* while being cut, or a person caught by Odieng. The elder is saying little more than that the ash is necessary, but he has not defined what the necessity is about.

The reference by another, in his speech at the end of Kombutsu, to the ash as "poison" is perhaps more suggestive. Commenting on this remark, one of my most perceptive informants alluded to a practice, which he felt was analogous, in which a warrior, who has become sick because he had seen too many persons bleed, will ritually eat something dirty or from a dirty bowl in order to become well. He also noted that a similar cure is prescribed for a person who suffers from bleeding feet: one eats again from a dirty bowl. A symbolic antipathy between certain forms of bleeding and dirt seems to permit dirt to be used to control bleeding. I have no other exegetical commentary on this opposition, or any other examples beyond those occurring in the initiation itself. That the initiates are not allowed to wash themselves or their cloths may be another expression of this principle, and so may be the ashen wine, the "poison." That also is something dirty.

The idea that the ash is a mode of control may also be interpreted more literally. By drinking the ash, do the initiates symbolically put back the blood they have shed? By putting back what they have lost, do the youth master the dangers of blood loss? On this point, there is an intriguing comparison with the initiation practices of the Bainouk, a people said to be the original inhabitants of the Casamance. My informants told me that these people actually pound the foreskins of the youth into a fine powder and drink a mixture of wine and powder at the end of their ritual.

Both the notions of dirt and replacement are apparently more explicit in the final act of Kombutsu, Bunoken (from *kanoken,* "to be dirty"), which I did not see. Sisa explained to me that in Bunoken the bull is killed to give back the blood which has been shed: "Their [the youths'] blood is shed. As we kill the cow, it's to say to the spirit to give back to them the blood which has been lost." The notion of replacement was prefigured at the ritual of Ichin, the small Kombutsu, which I described earlier in this chapter. Not only did the initiates face a representation of their own shed blood, but in the raw liver they ate a substance which prefigured the ash, or bull's blood, or both. At the same time, Bunoken may disclose other meanings as well. Elders told me that it was to "renew what is *munyo*," to "wash the heads" of the youth, and to "show Odieng the youth." None of these statements exclude the others or the idea of replacement, but it would have been necessary to have seen the ritual to formulate a better interpretation. It would be important to know, for example, and on this point I have conflicting testimony, whether the blood of the bull is given only to the initiates or is given to the spirit as well.[2]

Kombutsu, Souls, and Death

There are no funeral dances held during the initiation. Though several persons died during the months of the ritual, the mortuary ceremonies included none of the dancing and singing which usually embellishes them. This was true even for deaths of the old, when dancing is usually the most enthusiastic. The reason is that at the beginning of Kombutsu the village drums used in funeral dances were retired, as new drums were made to be played at the Kahus shrine. At the end of Kombutsu, these new drums become those played at funerals for the next generation.[3] When the initiates come out of the forest, not only will the drums of their ritual be those played at funerals, but they themselves will be participants as they have not been before. As I have noted, as "elders" (*abia*) they can see a cadaver without danger of Odieng. To see the sense of this prohibition, I want to place it in the context of other beliefs about, and avoidances of, death.

In several instances, women are separated from contact with the dead. For example, women still capable of producing children are forbidden to see the traditional tomb on penalty of "not being able to give birth." Again, if a young child (though not an infant) dies when its mother is not yet pregnant again, it is buried in a sitting position to prevent infertility in its mother. They bury the child, in other words, as if it were not really dead, for the dead are normally laid on their sides. An attempt seems to be made here to disguise the death of a child so that its death will not intrude on the mother's reproductive capacities or on the lives of children who follow. A stone or other marker is placed on top of its grave, for sometimes, when its mother is thereafter infertile, Ehing return to the grave to make sure the bones of the child have not inclined. If they have, they would be righted into a sitting position. A third custom separating the living from the dead concerns men as well as women. The living will change their names when someone with the same name dies at a young age.

In these practices, Ehing represent death as something contagious and something which obstructs fertility and life. The *munyo* governed by Odieng may be seen as a variant of this general idea: a "youth" (*ahula*), someone who has not shed sexual blood, is separated from death. But for *ahula,* this avoidance relates also to the logic of the cycle of souls. In formal terms, if not in actual fact, the death of an *ahula* implies the end of a line, for there would be no way for him to be reborn. Once an *ahula* has shed sexual blood, the social implications of death have altered, and with that alteration the danger represented by death vanishes. One recalls here the story that before men died, no one was born. Odieng's rule presents the corollary: that before Ehing die, they must give birth.

6

Widows

In the initiation, I have argued, men define their own powers by appropriating a sign of female sexuality. This definition occurs through Odieng's rules: in the rule that excludes women from Kombutsu and in the rule that requires an obligatory visit to Odieng's shrine to end the event. It is during this visit that the parallel between the blood of Kombutsu and the blood of birth is expressed most directly.

If this visit defines initiation and birth as parallel events, it also points to an asymmetry in the ritual obligations of men and women. For women, unlike the initiates, need not visit the shrine after they have given birth. Birth is followed, we have seen, by a period of ritual restriction, and this period is guarded by Odieng; but a visit to the spirit is not needed to end it.

There is, however, another rule of Odieng that involves a ritual obligation, and this rule is also asymmetrical. In this case, it is a rule that focuses on women and on the social transition associated with death rather than birth. A woman must visit the shrine after her husband's death and before engaging in relations with other men. But a widower is not subject to any direct involvement with the spirit. In this chapter, in which I take up this problem of the widow, I will show that, although the relations of asymmetry have shifted, the issue in both social transitions is the same.

Ewunyo—The Movement from Marriage

Immediately after her husband's funeral, a woman enters a period of transition known as *ewunyo*. This period marks the initial phase of separation between a deceased and living spouse; it is therefore seen as a parallel and an inversion of the period of *buwun* which inaugurates a marriage. Similar restrictions on behavior are in effect during both periods. As in *buwun*, a woman during *ewunyo* spends her day in a room of the house and departs briefly only in the early morning and evening. Like a bride, a widow may not work except to spin cotton. Again, both bride and widow are continuously provided with wine—the bride by her husband, the widow by her husband's brothers. But despite these behavioral similarities, there is an important difference in the moral condition of bride and widow. A widow directly after her husband's death is an ambiguous figure, and her ambiguity is conveyed through an additional restriction on her conduct. A widow observes all the taboos of a woman during menstruation and after birth, and, additionally, she is not allowed to eat meat sacrificed at a Kahin or the women's shrines of Baliga and Kaba. It is the moral quality of the widow, and the reasons for it, which led one individual to suggest that the word *ewunyo* is compounded from the roots of *buwun* (*-wun*), the period of seclusion that opens a marriage, and *munyo* (taboo). Although I am not able to evaluate this folk etymology on linguistic grounds, it does indicate the pronounced difference Ehing perceive between a bride and a widow.

Ewunyo lasts from two weeks to a month, and during this time a woman eats rice provided by her mother's brothers and by her husband's brothers. In contrast to a bride, who may be visited by anyone (except initially by her future husband) and especially by children, a widow is only seen by other persons who have previously lost a spouse. The secrecy which surrounds *ewunyo* centers on the ritual which terminates a widow's seclusion. I was not able to observe this ritual, but a cooperative elder described it just before I left the field. The widow is joined late at night by women of her own surname who have also been widowed. The women prepare a meal with the grain from the deceased's granary, which the wife eats. At dawn the women march in procession to the meander where the widow removes her clothing and is washed. Returning to the house, the women shave the widow's head. They then place a small libation pitcher on her forehead and rub her late husband's hatchet across

it saying, "Here is the hatchet (*odieng*) of your husband; today it's finished." Immediately after this ritual, the widow goes to Odieng's shrine.

At the death of a wife, a widower does not suffer the same restrictions
on his activity. However, at some point—any time from a month to a year
after his wife's death—he too will participate in a similar ritual. In this
instance, the man eats rice from his wife's granary and is rubbed with his
wife's weaving knife: "Here is the *esuum* of your wife; today it's finished."
The ritual is performed, again by women, but of the husband's clan
(patronym). Therefore, this ritual involves an extraordinary breach of
"cover" which otherwise separates the sexes: the women wash the naked
man at the meander. According to one elder, it is this breach which
accounts for the extreme secrecy of the ritual.

In each of these rituals the surviving spouse eats the rice of the dead,
setting up an image of attachment which is then broken or denied by the
rest of the rite: washing the body, shaving the head, and withdrawing an
instrument associated with the deceased's work. These acts communicate
a separation from the deceased spouse, and for a man this ritual is enough
to allow his return to normal life.

The Visits to Odieng

The death of a wife does not place a man in the same state as a widow.
Thus, only women must go to Odieng. There are two rituals, and they
are called Bune. The word *bune,* according to one of my best informants,
has the sense of "casting off a part of oneself"; he compared *bune* to the
verb *bule,* which refers to a snake changing skin or to removing an illness
from oneself by passing it on to another person. The name aptly characterizes the ritual action.

The rituals a widow performs differ significantly from the curing
ceremony at Odieng. The widow brings a small chicken and wine to the
shrine, but no rice. After she sits down with her back to the spirit, the
officiant places the chicken on top of her head and she begins to speak. If
the widow has not strictly observed the taboos associated with *ewunyo*—
for example, if she has sat on a stool—she asks the spirit's pardon; but
even if there has been no violation, she nevertheless says, "when I observed *ewunyo,* if I missed (*kapagun,* as a hunter "missing" a target),
pardon me." In other words, a confession is obligatory, and if there are no
specific and known breaches, she invokes the possibility that she might
have done something of which she is unaware. I was also told that a
woman might confess any forbidden knowledge she had gained during

her marriage: she and her husband might have "told each other things" in the privacy of their house and life together.

After the widow makes her speech, the priest cuts (*nasu*) the chicken's foot and then lets the fowl escape into the courtyard of his house. He pours the widow's wine into a small pot, takes a swallow, and spits it out on the woman's back. Afterward, he addresses the spirit: "She has come here as she lived with her husband. She has come, and that is our custom." In distinction to the ceremony for treating the sick, no wine is poured onto the spirit's shrine during this speech; as I was told, there is no "libating the taboos." The priest tells the widow to go away ("Now go until the day when you come to finish your speech"), and she leaves to wash in a pond.

When this ritual has been performed, the widow partially returns to a normal life. Several of the taboos are lifted—those concerning being "up high" (sitting on a stool, standing on a sill) and cooking—but she still may not have intercourse or eat the meat killed at a shrine. The prohibition on intercourse is lifted after the second ritual at Odieng which occurs several months to a year after her husband's death. This rite is distinctive. On this visit, the widow brings a rooster, wine, and rice to the shrine. The elder places an empty libation pitcher on her head, and she simply states that she has come to "finish her *bubane*" (*bubane*, "to perform a rite, arrange, gather things together for a trip"). The elder takes the rooster, kills it, and gives the widow a mixture of its blood and wine to drink. He spits pure wine on her back, and, as the second elder libates wine onto the shrine, he says "You heard, she says as she lived with her friend and as Iri has come for him, she came last time. She goes to her friend, she walks [*kaha,* the word used to denote a woman's marriage]." As in the other rituals at Odieng, the priest blows in the supplicant's ears and she departs.

Any interpretation of the two rituals should be predicated on the related ideas that the widow's visit to the shrine is obligatory and that she herself is not directly caught by Odieng but rather under the guard of the spirit. The obligation suggests that any confession which the widow might offer is secondary to the performance of the ritual, for the widow must visit even if she has not in actuality committed an offense. This requirement itself suggests that it is the social condition of the widow which is problematic.

When I asked various elders why a woman need visit Odieng but not a man, their consistent reply was that it was the woman who had "walked." Some persons went further to specify that the widow's ritual at Odieng "sweeps away" the ritual of "Holding Out the Spoon." This link between the two rituals is telling.

The convention of female walking, we have seen, defines a woman as the recipient of her husband's blood and a vehicle for his group's souls. Once a woman has taken a man's spoon and enters his house, all the children born to her will be his. This attachment to a husband becomes a source of ambiguity when he dies. Very simply, a woman is then defined as the recipient of the blood of a dead man, a man who is now physically absent. Before she can receive another man's blood, her continued attachment must be broken. Otherwise, the status of the father (pater) of any future children would inherently be in question. A woman must go to Odieng, it seems, not to separate herself from the spirit but from her husband before the spirit. As one elder put it to me, "You go to sweep away" the marriage.

The explicit purpose of the first ritual is to rid the widow of certain taboos, especially the interdiction on going "up high." The connection between this interdiction and her husband's blood is subtle and must be inferred both from the symbolic action and from other applications of this taboo. I have already noted that an interdiction on height is in effect during menstruation and during a period after giving birth. The same prohibition is also invoked and enforced by Odieng after the male initiates have been circumcised. In these contexts, height and bleeding are directly connected. Does this not imply, since the widow also cannot sit on stools or go up high into a granary, that she too, if not actually bleeding, is represented as if she were? Bleeding is, in fact, a curious feature in the rite.

In contrast to the curing ceremony, which begins with the patient talking into an empty libation pitcher, in this ritual the widow sits with the fowl on her head. She speaks of the restrictions on her behavior and of "things" she might have learned as a wife. Though this is not a confession in the same sense as that of an individual who has been "caught," I would still conclude that the import of placing an object above one's head is parallel. In both rituals, the gesture is used to transfer something away from one's self. The chicken in this instance is used to externalize an aspect of the widow's self rather than, as in the curing ceremony, to replace that part of the self that Odieng has taken. The fowl, in other words, is a vehicle to achieve a separation, a vehicle for the woman to dissociate herself from her experience as wife and as widow. The finality of this separation seems to be marked by cutting the chicken's toe: as the chicken bleeds, by implication it bleeds in place of the woman, for the taboo about height is terminated with the ritual.

If this is a plausible reading of the rationale and action of the ritual, it leads to a deeper question. Why is the widow represented as someone who bleeds? Here again I can only make an inference from the organization of the symbolism and from the link between the rituals that inaugurate and terminate sexual union. If a wife is socially defined as the recipient of a man's blood—the blood of intercourse used to represent the normative relationship—then she must lose blood to terminate the relationship. Her separation from her husband, and from herself as a wife, is achieved through a symbolic bleeding of his blood. And since she is not, as a widow, sensibly bleeding, the idea that she is bleeding can only be represented symbolically—that is, by invoking the taboos which hold when blood loss is actually present.

This sense of the rite, founded on the notion that a widow must remove her deceased husband's blood, is comparable to certain other beliefs and practices among the Kujumaat Diola. Sapir (1970: 1336) has described how, at the death of a spouse, rituals of washing and shaving rid the survivor of "past and now polluting body, blood, and semen contact with the deceased." In yet another ritual, this removal is graphic and parallels the idea that an Ehing widow bleeds out her husband's substance. The woman sits on the ground, legs apart. A slat from her husband's bed is placed between her legs; then it is removed and subsequently destroyed. The slat represents the deceased husband's penis (Sapir: personal communication).

Compared with the difficulties posed by the first visit to Odieng, the second seems straightforward. Until this ritual, the widow is still under the spirit's guard and still cannot have sex with another man. Or, as the Ehing say, only after the second ritual can a man "give her things to eat." The woman in this rite drinks rooster blood, a striking reversal of the limited identification of person and fowl brought about by using same sex blood at Odieng. As the elder of the shrine told me, "To finish the ritual of the husband, it's the rooster," which, he continued on another occasion, is "in place of her husband." With the consequences of the ritual in mind, I see this internalization of male blood as an act that reinitiates the woman's sexuality. The drinking of the blood prefigures the blood she is now permitted to receive. The widow's rite at Odieng separates the blood of a man from a woman and separates the blood of two men.

In the last chapter, I tried to show how Odieng's rules of separation define and celebrate the productive powers of men. From that point of view, the widow's ritual can been seen as a specification or application of the spirit's role in the initiation. The part that Odieng plays toward widows is to focus on blood as an idiom of reproductive rights—the spirit divides the claims of specific men from each other.[1] The initiation does not communicate these kinds of specific rights, but rather the general powers of men to create. Kombutsu, in other words, defines the powers that stand behind the specific rights that comprise the social structure. It is the ritual that conveys all that is meant in the notion of building a house.

Adultery and Divorce

The argument I have made about the widow and the organization of Odieng's rules provokes a comment about two other instances of social ambiguity—divorce and adultery. These occasions also involve a woman moving between two men, and yet neither is included in Odieng's prohibitions.

In three villages—Bakunum, Etafun, and Kuring—affairs with a married woman are formally forbidden. Such affairs are not condoned in the other villages, but they lack an explicit ideology which defines the prohibition. In these three villages, a man may also not have sex with a woman who divorced in his village. This rule may only be lifted if the former husband publicly renounces his wife. I was told he would climb a fan palm, tap loudly against its trunk, and announce the end of his claim to his wife.

In Bakunum, these prohibitions are attributed to the plight of a man named Ipialo.

> Ipialo was a small man. During the night while he slept his village mates would come and put Ipialo outside of his house in order to sleep with his wife. When Ipialo discovered what was happening, he called a village meeting to complain about the situation. Other men of the village agreed with him saying, "If a man marries a woman and she becomes available to everyone, we will be tired when war comes and not have the strength to fight." To avoid this, Ipialo decided to fix a shrine.
>
> So, Ipialo carried a basket of rice and a chicken to the meander. He was in the water a long time; then he said, "It's finished. Whenever a man sleeps with another's wife, he'll die."

I was told that because the shrine was planted in the water, its location remains hidden, and therefore no sacrifice is possible to confess a wrong-doing; as a result, villagers say the taboo is assiduously respected.

An elder from Etafun recounted a similar tale which justifies the taboo in his village:

> The youth slept with the wife of a small man. When the man complained to his friends, they told him to libate at a shrine where the men

libate after returning from war. But other men of the village told him not to libate until the youth arrived, for "they won't believe in the taboo and they'll die." But the man libated.

When the youth heard about it, they said that, since they weren't there, the taboo didn't apply to them. But whoever slept with another's wife died.

I was unable to obtain a story from Kuring.

Although these stories only mention adultery and not divorce, informants classed the two circumstances together, and the same stories are used to account for both proscriptions. In the Ehing villages that lack these rules, a distinction is made between a married and a divorced woman. Adultery in these villages often leads to conflict and sometimes to the breakup of a marriage. But intercourse with a divorced woman presents no problem whatsoever. Divorce is common in Ehing society[2]; it is described simply as a "separation" and no formal ceremony marks the event. There is no return of marital prestations.

The reason given in the Bakunum story for these rules about access to women is the necessity for male solidarity during fighting. One villager contended that the three villages have the taboos because they are situated on the border with the Diola village of Youtou with whom there had been wars in the past. But the Ehing have also warred with the neighboring Bayot and among themselves, and so this explanation does not adequately account for the particular geography of the taboos. Reference to war is again found in the Etafun story, where the taboo is initiated at the war shrine. Implied here is the idea that in war a village unites as a single moral community which must not be compromised by internal conflicts over women.

This idea links up with another, held by all Ehing, which also associates war with adultery. Ehing believe that if a man who sleeps with another's wife is wounded in battle, he will bleed to death if he comes in proximity to the cuckold. This belief may also be seen in the context of wartime solidarity, but it is interesting to note that the mode of death also bears resemblance to Odieng's affliction even though the spirit itself is not implicated.

What, then, can be said of these beliefs and Odieng's role? I suggested earlier in this chapter that a widow must visit Odieng to annul her status as the wife of a particular man, as the person who is socially defined as the carrier of his blood. Adultery, apparently, does not raise the same ambiguity in Ehing thought as does a husband's death. Even though a woman might literally receive the blood (semen) of a man not her husband, the latter still remains the social father of any child born and a consonance of blood and soul is maintained through a social fiction. There is no change of "father" as there will be when a husband dies.

Having said this, I want to make clear that Ehing do recognize a distinction between genitor and social father, and at certain times this distinction becomes socially relevant. When some infants are chronically sick, the situation may be traced to adultery. In these situations, Ehing say the child is crying because he is "not at the place where he was supposed to be born" and that the genitor has "lost his blood." To rectify the situation, the mother or a friend acting on her behalf must go "steal the salt" of the genitor. The salt is fed to the child and the mother says, "This is the salt of your father who gave birth to you." This statement is not true, but it is intended that, from the child's point of view, it be interpreted as true. It is intended, in other words, that by moving the salt of the genitor and giving it in the house of the father, the lack of congruence between substance ("blood") and house be redressed. The child will no longer cry for a lost father.

In the case of divorce, which is another kind of movement of women between men, there will be a change in "father." Why, then, does not a divorced woman, like a widow, need to go to Odieng? The simplest and most direct answer is that death and divorce are categorically distinct experiences. In a divorce the change of a father is preceded by a social separation. But a death brings about a physical separation that demands further definition. When death takes a spouse, the attachment of the couple still endures and calls for ritual that need not be invoked when the separation has taken place voluntarily.

PART III

Rain, Rice, and Land

The woman said: Giving birth is better than the initiation.

And then the man said: But your birth is dependent on us, on intercourse.

The woman: But for you to do the initiation, you must have children, birth.

The man: We will end your births by refusing sex, and we still will be able to carry on the initiation with those already born.

And here the woman taunts with the song: "They enter the bush like leopards, but come out treading so softly."

—Ehing folklore

7

The Meaning of Rice

When I began this study, I stressed the separation of the sexes as a key to understanding the structure of Ehing society. In their world, a system of classification orders social forms. The first part of this book has been an exploration of many basic features of Ehing notions of gender, especially the notions that define reproduction. In this exploration, we have seen that the concept of the "house" is crucial. Women must move to give birth in individual houses, and this movement is necessary because of the conceptual attachment of souls to land. In view of this attachment, the contrast between the locality of men and the movement of women is an idiom not only for the physical reproduction of individuals but for the social reproduction of groups. A house is a House.

We have also seen that the rules of Odieng order these ideas and practices about reproduction. The rule that separates youth from the dead communicates the logic of the cycle of souls. The rules that govern widows organize the rights that follow from the births that take place in individual houses. Most importantly, the rule that separates women from the initiation expresses the very powers men possess to build Houses, to build a cycle of descent.

Were the analysis to end here, Odieng would be seen as a power whose only function is to define male rights and powers. Its work is more complicated. As Odieng places a cloth around the initiation, the spirit does the same for birth, and it is the meaning of this rule that I now must investigate.

At the same time that I take up this aspect of Odieng's work, I also explore another feature of Ehing society involving women: their rights to land. At the beginning of this study, I introduced an anomaly in the Ehing system of land tenure—that women hold rights in land. This practice seems to violate a key component of lineage theory—that lineages are vehicles to regulate rights to the means of production. As Jack Goody (1973: 26) observes:

> In Africa, land is often inherited within a lineage or clan. When this happens, we can specify a certain tract of land as "belonging" to a particular group whose members have access to the uncultivated sections of that territory. The land passes by inheritance between members of the group, whether it is defined by matrilineal or patrilineal descent. . . . Using an ambiguous term in a very restricted way, we may speak of such descent groups as "corporate" when inheritance takes place within them, though clearly greater importance is to be attached to this designation if the property so transferred is the basic means of production, that is, land in an agricultural economy, livestock in a pastoral one.

In a patrilineal context, like that of the Ehing, one would expect that land, paralleling rights to group membership, would run down a line of men.

As I have stated, however atypical Ehing practice may be for patrilineal Africa as a whole, it should seem even more anomalous in the context of their own idioms, where descent is connected to men and land through the notions of souls. In this part of my study, I try to resolve this question about land, arguing that the anomaly in the system of land tenure makes sense in terms of Odieng's work and the understanding of women that follows from it. In other words, I argue that an understanding of the taboo on birth provides an understanding of the system of inheritance.

As a clue to this analysis, I return again to the marriage tale. In the marriage tale, God (Iri) finally brought the man and woman together in his modality as rain. Although the text stresses that the union of the sexes was to produce a child, the story also evokes the other important product of men's and women's work: rice. For it is during the rainy season that men and women combine their labors in farming. Rice, then, is my point of departure to explore the Ehing conception of female rights and the meaning of the rule that covers a birth.

Rice cultivation in the Casamance represents a subtle and complicated ecological adaptation. It is a subject in itself (see, in this regard, the works of Pélissier 1966, and Linares 1970, 1981), and my presentation of the Ehing variant of this adaptation can hardly be considered exhaustive. What I focus on here is the form of labor performed by men and women. My point in describing this labor is to make and illustrate one simple point: the specific way in which women's work in the fields is essential and valued. Women possess their own land and possess their own granaries, and these rights are coextensive with the role women play in farming. From this description of work, I then trace the social implications of women's work in the fields. I shall show that a description of women's work leads to a consideration of a more comprehensive conception of female productive capacity, a conception of women's rights and powers that is symbolized through rice.

The Ecology of the Casamance

To understand the details of rice production, one must have some sense of the Ehing habitat. The Casamance River dominates the topography of the region to which it gives its name. The river bisects the region as it winds its way to the Atlantic and is fed by a series of tributaries—what geographers call meanders—which cut through the land. These meanders create a complex design of gradual slopes and depressions and lend an ecological subtlety to what otherwise appears as remarkably flat terrain. These meanders become progressively smaller as their distance increases from the river; at their farthest extension, they become simple gutters filled only during the rains.

The river rises and falls with the daily movement of the Atlantic tides and with the alternation of rainy and dry seasons. The salty water and tides of the sea penetrate for more than 60 miles inland, up the river and out into the smaller meanders which border the villages, creating brackish wetlands.

In the past, Ehing carved out paddy fields from the mangrove swamp, right up against the meander. But since the diminution of rains in this part of West Africa, the people have abandoned these fields, and concentrate their efforts on the plains that lie between the swamp and the upland of the villages proper. These plains are poorly drained and quickly become inundated during the rains. They are well suited for rice. The soil is sandy and porous near the upland but becomes progressively richer and clayey as it nears the meander, where it remains wet for several months after the rains have ceased. The water running off the upland each year helps restore the soil, but Ehing also fertilize their fields. Cattle are pastured on the fields during the dry season, and traditionally women scattered ash prepared from household debris over their land. Today some individuals buy fertilizer directly from the government.

The Ehing year is oriented toward the arrival of the rains. The rains begin in early June. At first there are sporadic thunderstorms, just hints of the coming monsoons, which help break up the grueling heat of March, April, and May—when, as Ehing say, "you can almost touch the sun." These first rains wash off the layers of dust that by then cover much of the vegetation. By July the rains are frequent, and during August it rains almost every day. (In August 1976, it rained twenty-eight days; as my thatch roof was in ill repair, I happened to have kept count.) Thereafter, the rain slowly diminishes and usually ends by October. Ehing are much concerned about the duration and plenitude of the rains. According to government measurements, precipitation has been as little as 831 mm and as much as 1,161 mm in any one year. This variation results in harvests of relative scarcity and plenty. Elders repeatedly told me that the rains today, even in good years, are not what they were during their youth before the chronic drought in West Africa, when the season began in May rather than June and also lasted longer.

With the rains comes relief from heat but also the mosquitoes. The wet, open paddy fields make ideal breeding grounds; the hum of these insects is constant and loud indoors at night, punctuated by hands slapping and dogs growling. Malaria is endemic among the people, and during the rainy season many suffer from frequent and sometimes severe attacks. The most pleasant part of the year falls between November and February, when the mosquitoes are all but gone, the air is fresh, and the nights are cool enough to draw the Ehing to their morning fires for warmth.

The reversal of the seasons—"the rains" (*karui*) and "the heat" (*ole*)—is the most conspicuous feature of the climate. Ehing themselves divide the year into seven seasons whose names are associated either with features of weather or with activities (such as harvesting) which take place at that time.

Cultivating

Like other peoples, the Ehing possess several stories which relate that their hard work in the fields is made necessary by an unfortunate error. In one of these stories, Atunen, the ancestor or "first person," had wanted to tell the people that if they were to put just one single grain of rice in a clay pot, it would become full of grain. Atunen sent Erutu (I think a species of heron) to show people this procedure, but Erutu was not listening carefully to what Atunen had said. So when he reached the people, Erutu said, "Atunen said to take a 'measure' of rice and put it in this pot. It will become full, and you will be able to eat until next year." Because of Erutu's mistake, the people have to work hard to fill their granaries, and still there is sometimes not enough.

As this tale implies, Ehing farming is demanding—a process of cultivating, transplanting, and harvesting. But despite the note of lament, the people approach their work with industry and enthusiasm. To a large extent, a family of husband, wife, and unmarried children compose an independent economic group. Within the family, men and women perform well-defined, separate tasks, but labor is cooperative in the sense that spouses engage in complementary work on each other's land. To cultivate, a man uses a long-handled fulcrum hoe with a wooden scoop capped with an iron blade. This hoe, which Ehing call *kapes* (and Diola, *kajando*), is unique to the populations in the northernmost extension of the West African wet-rice belt. In her agricultural tasks, a woman works with a small knife to harvest the crop and with a heavy pestle and mortar to process the grain.

In farming, as in the production of most traditional staples in West Africa, there is a complex interdigitation of sexual roles, to borrow Jane Guyer's apt description (Guyer 1984: 383). Ehing mark, and even celebrate, these roles in ritual, often employing, as we saw in the funeral rituals, the tools associated with male and female work.

The agricultural year begins before the rains, in late March, when men clear the tracts to be used as nurseries. For approximately two months, though not every day, they hack away at bush and undergrowth with their machetes; only the palms and larger trees are left standing. Several sites may be cleared each season, and these are located on the upland, some adjacent to houses and others deeper in the bush. The size of an individual's nursery varies considerably and depends on such factors as how densely seeds are broadcast and the measure of an individual's paddy fields. Half a hectare seems common. Ehing make certain to have more seedlings than they need for their fields; any excess is left to rot, or is given as a gift to elder relatives. Once used, a nursery site will lie fallow three to six years.

The burning of the cut foliage, which occurs by early June, leaves a thin layer of ash on the ground. Women may help weed out any roots or plants that escaped the fire. The trunks of the palms are simply scarred, and Ehing sometimes use the height of the mark to judge the age of a particular fallow.

Since women store the seed during the year, they bring varieties of rice to the nursery, but their husbands do the actual broadcasting. The men sprinkle seed in rows of about a meter in width and with their hoes toss on a thin cover of soil. Within a nursery, distinct sections are reserved for different varieties or rice—each with different properties and matura- tion periods—and the seeds of husband and wife are planted in distinct areas.

Sowing takes about a month to complete. Ehing start to sow after the first rains, usually by mid-June, but sometimes as late as the first week of July. They want to broadcast early enough in the season so that the plants will not be caught short of water in the paddy fields; but they also want to be sure that the rains have begun in earnest before risking the seed. Each individual makes his own decision to begin, though everyone seems to start within a few days of each other. The decision is something of a point of competition. In the past, I was told, some individuals began their work secretly at night, as if to get ahead of their neighbor. I was once asked whether someone I knew well had begun to broadcast, and, when I answered truthfully that he had not, I could sense that my response was greeted with some skepticism.

In early August, as the plains between the upland and the mangrove swamp begin noticeably to hold water, men begin to "cultivate" (eya). The people have used their hoe technology to develop an intensive agri- culture based on rainwater rather than irrigation. To capture water and retain water levels, Ehing have divided the plains into a multitude of plots each surrounded by a small bund. The size of these parcels, some rec- tangular and some irregularly shaped, vary from a few to several hundred square meters. In any village, these plots may number in the thousands; to an outsider they appear as a vast maze in which it is easy to become lost. Ehing do little else to manage water. A few natural channels that run from plateau to meander are kept clear and are periodically used, especially at the beginning of the work season, to evacuate any excess water from the paddy fields; as necessary, men simply slash open bunds leading to the channel. Sometimes bunds are slashed to share water, but this practice is infrequent since all depend on the same rains. Conflict over water, in any event, is minimal. Water remains in the fields well beyond the harvest, and, as I have already noted, it is several months after the rains have ceased before the deeper areas of the plain are dry.

Men prepare the plots to receive the seedlings (Fig. 7.1), making rows of ridges and furrows. Each year, beginning about mid-August, Ehing open the ridges of the previous crop, and, capturing old roots and stalks, they build ridges out of last year's furrows. With this method, water fills the furrows and spreads evenly over the ridges; hence, it is constantly available to the rice roots without endangering the rest of the plant. The fields in the village are divided into several categories of land which are

Fig. 7.1. In two adjacent plots, fathers and sons prepare the rice fields with hoes (*kapes*).

based mainly on soil type. Ehing work the sandy, more porous ground near the upland early in the season, and it is to this ground that women will later transplant the fastest growing varieties of rice. Men turn to the more retentive soils of the bottomland later in the season, and these will receive the slower maturing, but more fecund, varieties. As men proceed to cultivate each category of land, they attend to their own fields before those of their wives. A summary of land categories, including the deep fields of the mangrove which are no longer worked, is given in Table 7.1. Speaking for the Diola, Linares (1981: 563) has suggested that "the highly localized nomenclature applied to field classification reflects the Diola peasants' inability to modify in any extensive way the local topography." This would hold true for the Ehing as well.

The labor demands of cultivating are visibly marked by the shrinking stomachs of the men. They work between six and eight hours a day and for a season which, depending on land resources, lasts for several months. The fields cultivated by Ehing are not contiguous. Although a majority of an individual's plots may be found in the fields of the village in which he was born, they are scattered. Moreover, all persons hold rights to land in several villages other than their own. This fragmentation of holdings is obviously adaptive in a monocultural setting where rainfall and crop disease may differ even in neighboring locations. At the same time that it

TABLE 7.1
Ehing Land Categories

Meander (*otis*)

   bunyo   Deeply flooded fields, with bunds up to 1 meter, cut from the mangrove swamp. Periodically flushed to desalinize soil, irrigated with water from the meander. Ehing began to work these fields before the rains but transplanted seedlings near the end of the season. Rich soils produced the most abundant yields. No longer cultivated.

Rain-Fed Fields (*buriame*)

   kafies   Adjacent to meander, this land was traditionally not cultivated but was an area where women gathered salt. Some paddy fields today.

   kaiis   Beginning of clay soils (moving from meander). Medium deep bunds, the zone after *kasian* to receive seedlings.

   kuguo   The lowest fields, with bunds up to half a meter. Rich, clayey soil. The last fields to be prepared each season, receive the most productive varieties of rice.

   kagis   Traditionally part of *kagis* was set aside for thatch but is now cultivated to take up the loss of *kasian*. Shallow fields.

   kasian   Sandy soils, and small plots with low bunds. The first land each season to be worked. Sometimes Ehing broadcast seed directly here. Much *kasian* is given to women.

   iribun   Land between fields and upland, used to pasture cattle and some secondary crops. Never cultivated.

Upland (*bure*)   Land of the central plateau. Homogenous palm forest, site of houses and nurseries.

Forest   To Ehing, forest is the original covering of the land, now found only toward the frontier with Guinea-Bissau.

---

reduces risk, however, a distribution of an individual's fields adds to labor, especially to that of the women who must carry seedlings during transplanting and grain during the harvest.

Ehing transplant rice for sound ecological reasons: seed is economized, yields are better, and young plants are less vulnerable to weeds and insects. Some four to six weeks after sowing, women pull seedlings by their roots and usually store a basketful overnight before carrying them the next day to the paddy fields. There, each plant is individually placed in the ridges, and varieties with different properties are coordinated to different soils.

Women are also responsible for the harvest. Rice ripens from the end of October through January; harvesting begins in December and lasts into February. Each plant is cut individually with a small knife and these are then gathered into bunches (*openye*) and allowed to dry in the sun. The work is extremely tedious and back-breaking, made harder by the glare of the sun reflected off the water in the fields. Headaches and irritation are common. A friend jokingly confided that he is always careful what he says to his wife during this season, because she "gets angry over anything." Some men, with particularly abundant fields, may offer sporadic help with harvesting. But mostly they watch over the ripe crop and, with children, try to chase away the weaver birds.

Women transport the rice to the house in large baskets balanced on their heads. Before the rice is put in the granaries, the husband designates which bundles he will use as seed for next year's crop. A woman husks this rice and follows suit with her own. The harvest is then put in the couple's respective granaries, located in the sleeping rooms of the house.

In the course of a season, some families need additional help. Ehing must work their fields and tend their crops within the time limits of the rainy season, and the balance of land and labor in any particular family may make this impossible. Furthermore, communal work is sometimes more pleasant, and the quick completion of particular fields may help maturation and harvesting schedules (Linares 1970). However, I should stress that this labor is recruited on an ad hoc basis and that families may solicit help one year and not another. Some Ehing have never joined in the reciprocal arrangements through which labor is allocated. Male labor was traditionally pooled from several sources—patrilineal kinsmen, coresidents, and friends—and any one of these might contribute one or two days of cultivating in any season. Women also formed associations of coresidents or friends who helped each other transplant and harvest.

Traditionally, an individual who gained help would be expected to work in turn for others and, in addition, to provide a basket of rice from the harvest for the group's collective consumption. It was not uncommon for kinsmen or friends to eat the afternoon meal together for several weeks. When women help a man's wife, he will often give them wine as well to supplement the rice. Today, money is the more usual payment, and the traditional reciprocal system of aid is breaking down. Instead, village men and women of the same age form groups to help each other and to hire out on a contract basis. Larger groups (for example, all the bachelors of a village, or even all its able-bodied men) work and keep their earnings in collective funds.[1]

Ehing are conservative with their rice, carefully measuring the allotment for each meal, and they frequently talk about the prospects of the rains, the harvest, and the possibility of being "caught by hunger." As a people, they are familiar with both lean and plentiful harvests, and this alternation may account for how tenaciously they conserve—even hoard—grain in their granaries. The crop itself is kept as bundles in baskets, and, as Ehing do not maintain any count of these, it is impossible for me to give an accurate measure of their stocks. To the people the measure of a granary is qualitative—for example, it is "full" or "depleted." Today they complain that in general their stock is not what it once was, when the surpluses of each year eventually built up an ample accumulation of "old rice." I was told that ten-year-old rice, reddened with age and perhaps barely edible, was once not uncommon. I did see some granaries with rice almost that old. A well-stocked granary, hinted at but never publicized, is a source of prestige for a family.

Other families seem barely to meet their subsistence needs and each year are forced to buy rice from merchants in Ziguinchor who import it from abroad. Several factors contribute to these differences in wealth. Some Ehing have not received enough land through inheritance to support themselves adequately. Pélissier (1966: 759) has estimated the rice yields in the Casamance at some 900 kg of milled rice per hectare, which means that a family with several children must put about three-quarters of a hectare under cultivation.[2] Those with less land than is needed may attempt to borrow to make up the difference; one friend of mine with three small children, for example, received only about 4,000 square meters as his inheritance and then borrowed some 9,000 square meters from his maternal uncle. Elders with married children tend to need less land and may loan areas to either descendants or uterine kin.

Access to land alone, however, does not condition plenitude or scarcity; there is a second factor. Though most Ehing labor intensively, a few are "lazy." There is a proverbial insult reserved for such men: "He cultivates from morning to night but only finishes three plots." Such individuals may find difficulty in either attracting or keeping a spouse, for women do not want to marry where they will be hungry. Finally, many contingent events may influence the stock in a granary. For example, fathers usually support their sons through the first years of marriage, but a son who marries after his father has died will not benefit from this start in life. Various rituals also require great expenditures of rice, especially rituals for children's rites of passage and the male initiation, and some individuals suffer more than others from the timing of these events.

Before imported rice could be bought at Ziguinchor, poor men would solicit help from their wealthier kinsmen. Help was always asked in secret, for not to have enough rice to feed the family is "shameful"; conversely, the donor of the rice was forbidden to make public mention of the recipient. Moreover, no person would admit to being rich. Though wealth in rice is, as I noted, prestigious, it may also be a source of tension, as it provokes jealousy. A wealthy man never admits to his fortune, therefore, to avoid the ill-will of others and also to avoid raising questions about how the surplus was obtained, for Ehing believe that one may exchange the souls of children with bush spirits in return for a good crop. These suspicions may become especially rife among close kin who, living in proximity, can assess each other's fortune and be provoked to *odzimo*, "jealousy."

Men's Rice and Women's Rice

The work in farming is cooperative and complementary. But all this cooperative labor does not result in a common store of rice. On the contrary, the crop itself is kept strictly separate; husband and wife control their own harvest. To even look into a spouse's granary requires permission.

This point about separate granaries cannot be overemphasized. This practice connects the technical labor I have just described to the larger issue of notions of sexual classification. I want to argue that the right of women to their separate crop expresses the value of women's labor. This value of labor—and indeed, the value of the whole role of women in production and reproduction—is symbolized through rice.

Eating among the Ehing centers around rice; the very word for meal, *imiip*, is the same as for "cooked rice." Families eat rice at every meal and from a common bowl. Men and teenage males typically eat with spoons, whereas women and other children eat with their hands.[3] Often the rice is covered with palm-oil sauce and, less frequently, supplemented with carp or other local fish. Sometimes a family will of necessity eat plain rice, *kadie*, but with no great enthusiasm. Currently, most Ehing eat three meals a day, and I would estimate that a family of six consumes about two kilograms of milled rice daily. In the past, women reputedly ate only two meals to conserve rice; and children, in the time before local education, would miss the noon meal as they spent their days at the meander looking for fish.

Women are the cooks, except when they are out in the fields from morning to night during the harvest. Bundles of paddy are taken down from the granaries about once a week. Women thrash the paddy with a dance-like movement of their feet, set the grain out in the sun to dry, and then pound it with pestle and mortar. Sometimes mother and daughter, or co-wives, pound together.

Both husband and wife share responsibility for feeding the family. At the end of the harvest, when the rice has been transported into the house, a husband offers his wife one basket of rice called a "hand." She prepares the family meal with this rice, which may last several weeks, and then announces she will begin to serve her own grain. This period of eating female rice is called *bali*. *Bali* begins sometime in January and lasts between two and four months, until her grain is finished.

When a woman tells her husband that her crop is depleted, it probably does not mean that the crop of that year is actually exhausted. A prudent woman always keeps some rice in reserve which, in the event that her marriage is terminated, she will transport to her father's or brother's house and use for her meals. A husband may challenge the duration of his wife's contribution, and I was told that, if a woman's crop seemed to be finished prematurely, a husband may suspect his wife of hoarding and refuse thereafter to cultivate her land. In a polygamous household, wives jointly contribute their rice to the family bowl and may cook together; sometimes there is competition between co-wives to see whose rice lasts longer. A husband with more than one wife benefits in the sense that less of his own crop is consumed.

A man's contribution to the bowl begins at the end of *bali*. There is no special name given to this period. A man's grain may last through the next year's harvest, at which point he will put away any surplus and begin eating the new crop. However, if the family's grain is in short supply during the harvest, the woman each day will take home a bundle of paddy from whatever field she happens to be working in.

Except for a few ritual occasions, a family eats its own rice. If other persons arrive during a meal, they will always be invited to "eat"— *oringo*—and they will customarily refuse. It is considered improper to encroach on another family's grain. Ehing level an insult at those who think more of their stomachs than of this propriety: "He sees the smoke (of cooking) and enters (the house)."

The exclusivity of rice sometimes also extends to other foods and objects, both within the house and without. Two simple examples convey these conventions better than a formal statement. I once asked a research assistant from another village who was visiting to join me at a ceremony in the village in which I lived, but he refused, saying that some might think he was in attendance only for the wine which would be drunk after the libation. In a second instance, a friend, the head priest of Odieng, once brought me a gift of bananas wrapped in cloth during a village gathering. He pulled me aside to present the gift; when I began to unwrap the fruit to give back his cloth, he protested that I could give it back later. Otherwise, he said, others would see precisely what I was holding and would be able to make demands on the fruit. In the context of these conventions, a house represents a very general and enduring boundary which makes what lies within it into an object that is socially invisible.

But if Ehing respect each other's hearths, they also give many gifts.

They treat strangers generously and graciously. They are certain either to find fish or to kill a chicken whenever a stranger arrives. Often visitors will be given their meal in a separate bowl as a sign of respect and so that they do not have to contend with the subtle process of sharing the same rice; alternatively, on these occasions, the men will eat separately from women and children.

Rice and Separation

The combination of labor in farming—the union to produce rice as well as children—is given expression in a ritual I have already described, the marital rite of "Holding Out the Spoon." Recall that in this ritual the couple receives rice together at the Kahin shrine—offered by a married female relative. The meaning is quite direct: just as they will mix their blood in intercourse, husband and wife will participate together in work and will eat from a common bowl. The act of offering rice on a spoon obviously gives the ritual its name. The couple shares the same rice from the same spoon. Since women normally do not eat with spoons, with either traditional wooden spoons or steel imports, their receiving rice on a spoon is a marked usage which dramatizes the commensality that begins with marriage.

That both husband and wife are fed also foreshadows the practice that the couple will eat parental rice for the next several years. For two years, father and son cultivate their fields together, as they had done before the marriage; but both families will eat the rice which comes from the elder's fields. The younger couple will store all the crop coming from its own land, and the people remark that this enables the younger generation to get a start on life. During the dry season after the second harvest, the son builds his house. Father and son cultivate together for a third season, but with that harvest the couple, having moved into its own house, begins to eat its own rice.

Still, even though the younger couple eats parental rice for two years, they do not eat with the elders out of a common bowl. Rather, their marriage inaugurates a set of food avoidances between the generations. The breaking of these taboos produces an illness called *kulio* (*olio,* "to cook"), the symptom of which is diarrhea which "comes out of the body like the boiling water in a cooking pot." There are two prohibitions:

1. A married woman cannot eat out of the same bowl with either her husband's father or mother.
2. A man may not eat out of the same bowl with his mother-in-law (but is permitted to do so with his father-in-law).

Kulio only attacks the person of the older generation. Interestingly, rice may be passed to the younger couple, but leftovers from the children's bowl cannot be eaten by parents. These food taboos continue even after the couple has set up its own separate household.

The people's explanation of *kulio* is a pragmatic one: in their view, the rules serve to prevent an intrusion on the younger generation's rice. Since parents have more or less unchecked authority over their children, the argument goes, they could make unlimited demands on their grain, were it not for the taboos. At any time, they could join a meal in progress and a child could hardly refuse. And since authority is unidirectional, so are the rules: the younger generation, with no authority, can take leftovers, but the reverse is not allowed.

As if to persuade me of this interpretation, villagers in Bakunum pointed to the tensions in the household of Martin Sagna. At the time of my fieldwork, Martin was about thirty years old and lived with his widowed mother and two younger brothers. For some years, Martin's mother had complained publicly that none of her sons had yet found a wife. Martin's status also concerned the elders of his House. I was told by observers of the situation that the problem stemmed from the brothers' laziness in the fields—no woman would want to live a life of hunger. But in 1976, Martin's youngest brother impregnated a woman. Several months before she was to give birth, she came to live in Martin's house. Within a short time, serious tensions surfaced between mother and daughter-in-law. The old woman was quick to criticize, and matters came to a head when the moment of birth approached. One of the important roles of a mother-in-law is to assist in the delivery of her grandchild, but, on the day the younger woman went into labor, Martin's mother was nowhere to be found. She had gone visiting. The gossip: "She said she wanted her sons to marry; well, where was she?" And the explanation: "She really did not want her sons married, because then she could no longer share their bowl."

We might put this indigenous explanation in more abstract terms. At marriage, the generations are separated economically, and *kulio* is a symbolic idiom which expresses and maintains this separation. Some of my informants, however, went further in their explanations and connected the specific pattern of the rules to possible modes of residence. A man's parents may not eat with his wife, but only a mother-in-law may not eat with her daughter's husband. *Kulio* is not present when a man shares a bowl with his son-in-law. And why the asymmetry? According to native exegesis, *kulio* is present between a woman and her in-laws because there are ample opportunities for the generations to eat together. In contrast, a man will never live with his father-in-law, and so there could never be chronic demands for rice. He might, however, live with his mother-in-law, for she might come to live with her daughter on divorce or the death of a husband.

A Comparative Note

Questions may be raised about this exegesis, for it seems a bit strained and ad hoc. There may be other latent meanings in *kulio* besides the functional one which Ehing propose and which makes *kulio* a strictly utilitarian device. This possibility is suggested by a similar, but more extensive, set of rules among the neighboring Kujumaat Diola (Diola-Fogny) which has been analyzed by J. David Sapir.

The rules are governed by a spirit called *Kujaama*. Like *kulio*, *Kujaama* also enforces a rule about parents eating from the same bowl as their married children. But it will also catch an elder, male or female, who touches a daughter during her menstruation or who comes too close to a daughter while she is giving birth. Furthermore, at a funeral the surviving spouse must go through rituals to avoid *Kujaama*, and these involve treating rice from the deceased's granary. A more complex representation than *kulio*, *Kujaama* communicates a principle of separation with respect to sexuality as well as food. To the Diola, rice and blood are, in fact, inextricable, and sexuality lies at the heart of the native model:

> To the Fogny the idea of *Kujaama* is explained by their theory of blood flow. Blood passes from one generation to the next and mixes during sexual intercourse. . . . Blood flow from an older to a younger generation should be irreversible. . . . The Fogny say that at marriage blood extends to include cooked food. Thus, as a man and his wife mixed their blood through intercourse, so their joint labor creates mixed produce.
>
> . . . To reverse the blood is to mix blood between generations. Where this occurs, the elder suffers pollution, for it is he who sustains the mixture: his own blood mixed with blood "returned," that is, blood he has already passed on. Nothing happens to the younger for he only passes back what he has received. For these reasons to touch or to receive something directly from a menstruating daughter or a daughter who is a new mother and is still "wet" brings back, or reverses, the blood to form the polluting mixture. In the same way, to eat food that has touched the mouth of one's married child brings the same results. (Sapir 1970: 1336)

Sapir concludes this section of his analysis with the observation that "all forms of intergenerational *Kujaama* pollution boil down to acts of symbolic incest between parent and child."

Is *kulio* a code for sexuality as well? Diola ethnography strikes a familiar chord: for Ehing, also, male and female labor combine to produce rice (although the crop is kept separated) and a man and woman mix their blood. This conjoining is conveyed in the marriage ritual we have been examining. But the Diola have made an explicit parallel between rice and blood in terms of intergenerational rules; the Ehing have structured their ideas differently. Though I suspect a sexual implication to *kulio,* the notion remains undeveloped. Avoidances having to do with blood have nothing explicitly to do with generations and are ordered by Odieng rather than *kulio.* What we find here is a resemblance of ideas that have been subjected to different organization, common symbols that take different forms like the elements, to borrow Lévi-Strauss's (1960: 36) image, through the turns of a kaleidoscope.

Rice and Idioms of Maternal Production

Whatever the meaning of *kulio,* rice is used in other social and ritual contexts as well. I will now document these uses and how they enter into the idiom of "giving birth" that is the cultural rubric of female labor.

A mother is charged with the initial social and ritual responsibilities for a child's care. In the first year or two of life, a child eats rice only from his mother's granary. For several days after birth, a child is fed a farina made from three- or four-year-old rice, for the people believe that fresh rice is unhealthy for an infant. The farina is made from the rice a woman brought with her when she married. When the child begins to eat cooked rice, he or she does so apart from the family bowl; at mealtime, a mother gives her child rice in a small, separate bowl. Any rice left over from this bowl is saved and offered to the child sporadically throughout the day. Usually before a child is two years old, his father calls him over to begin eating at the family bowl; but in some households a mother will continue to feed the infant until she has her next child.

Women are also the central figures in protecting children. In the Casamance infants are often ill, and their mortality figures are very high. There are various rituals that seek to protect them. Within the first month or two of life, a child is taken by its mother to a spirit named Ibun (from *bubun,* "medicine"). A ceremony is performed at the shrine, the purpose of which is to prevent diarrhea and coughing, two of the most common childhood ailments. The spirit has a protective role and apparently is thought to stay with the child, for several months later a second ritual is performed which "returns Ibun." There are several Ibun shrines, though the spirit is not represented in each village. A woman takes her child to the same shrine where she herself was taken by her own mother. Ibun, then, organizes a tie between mothers and daughters which is based on their role as bearers of children from generation to generation. Though men may act as priests at an Ibun shrine, fathers are excluded from the rituals of their own children.

As women have the primary responsibility for the early care of children, they also attend to the deaths of the very young. These children are often not accorded funerals but are buried without ceremony in the bush, for Ehing believe that sometimes they do not have souls and hence are not persons but "something." Alternatively, the child's soul has by accident entered into the wrong House and so has returned into the earth. The judgment whether a child warrants a funeral is made by older women who are no longer capable of reproduction. The body is carried out by the husband's married female agnates; as one woman explained, this may be seen as a continuation of their role which began with the "covering" of the mother's stomach. The mother herself in these instances is a sad bystander as the child is placed in a shallow grave.

In many cases, the deaths of children are attributed to witchcraft. Children are thought to be easy prey. Witches are thought to take their souls, making them sick, and to keep them hidden away. To cure a child, a parent may ask a curer to go on a search for a soul. In especially acute or chronic cases, all the women of a village may gather together to go on such a hunt. They seek the soul in the houses, and they seek to liberate it from a bedroom (where it is usually found) by breaking through the wall of the room with a pestle.

Ironically, the witches are often, though not always, found to be women. Ehing assume a tendency of women to compete over children. Children embody female accomplishment in this culture, and women are thought likely to be jealous of each other's offspring as men are of each other's land and harvest. This attribution fits in with the case I discussed in Chapter 3, in which Alfred moved away from his father's house because his children were sick and because this sickness was attributed to a rancor between the men's wives. Recall, also, that the word for "co-wives" is also the word for enemies. This is a structural assignation. Clearly, many co-wives get along famously, and women often encourage husbands to take second wives, particularly to help with labor. If one woman constantly sneaks sand in the cooking rice of her peer, another pair are fast friends. But, as a structural fact of their society, Ehing believe that the enemies of children are always close at hand; a woman who loses many children will move away to protect her offspring.

Perhaps the most dramatic expression of this attribution to women is found in the beliefs Ehing hold about breast milk. Ehing explain that a woman's first milk is "dirty." This description is their characterization of colostrum, the yellowish or amber milk secreted for a few days after childbirth. In their view, the milk has been made "dirty" by a jealous woman who comes "during the night" to nurse at an expectant mother's breasts and leaves a poisonous residue. As a result, a woman's first milk is "bloody" and, if she were to nurse her child, he would die. To eliminate this danger, the mother visits a curer about three days after delivery (when, in fact, colostrum turns to breast milk) who "pulls out what is dirty inside" and verifies that the redness in the milk has disappeared.

The jealous woman who comes in the night is always thought to be someone close at hand, though no actual person is ever named as the cause of the bad milk. But she is assumed to be either a co-wife or the wife of anyone else in the House.

Uterine Kin

In the last section, I noted some of the responsibilities and attributes of women that derive from their role in "giving birth." Though not all of these are positive, all reflect forms of women's rights and powers. Now "giving birth" (kabosu) is more than the physical act of delivery—in the social thought of the Ehing it is also an idiom of relationship. The idiom conveys the relationship between an individual and various relatives to whom he is related through uterine links. These relatives are called kumumen. Kumumen are persons who are members of the Houses of one's mother, mother's mother, father's mother, and mother's "fictive brother."[4]

An individual may address any female member of these four Houses, irrespective of generation, nunindze (literally, "my mother"). Any male member of these Houses is called mumeninzde. A translation of kumumen as "uterine kin" appears to correspond closely to the meaning of the term.

Kumumen say they have given birth to the "children" of their sisters. To point out an individual, any uterine relative might say, "there is our child; we gave birth to him." Furthermore, this notion of birth is associated with milk. A "child" of kumumen is a sibling of anyone else with whom he shares these relatives; but, in contrast to the "siblings" of the same House, with whom he shares land, he and uterine-linked persons are said to share milk ("our milk is one"). Free of the ambivalences which inhere in coresidence, it is an especially supportive and free relationship. Of course, this is a characteristic feature of uterine relationships in patrilineal Africa.

Coupled with the notion that uterine kin "give birth" and are con-

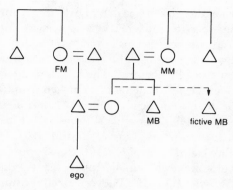

Fig. 7.2. Uterine kin.

nected in that way to sisters' children is an idiom of "possession" (*kasi*). However, this idiom is more restricted than that of birth. It is used to define the ties between an individual and his mother's House and that of her fictive brother, but not to *kumumen* of the generation of grandparents. The mother's House is said to "possess the head" of a sister's child ("we possess his head, we gave birth to him") and her other "brother's" House to "possess his legs." These designations refer to the division of a cow sacrificed at a sister's child's funeral by his agnates; the top half of the cow is given to the mother's natal House and the lower half to the House of the fictive brother. The cow "pays" the uterine kin for the woman they provided to bear their group a member—a payment for reproductive rights.

From an individual's perspective, *kumumen* and House comprise the two primary categories of his social world. The idioms which convey relationships with uterine kin, "birth" and "possession," together define manifold rights, claims, and obligations.

As might be anticipated for a West African society, a sister's child, whether male or female, has the right to "snatch" things belonging to his *kumumen*. In recognition of this right, uterine kin, besides calling a sister's child "child" (*ashiam*), will call him *asebun*. In fact, *asebun* is the most frequently used reciprocal of "my uterine relative." The term derives from the verb *kasebun*, "to take something freely" and, to the best of my knowledge, is used only in the context of taking property from *kumumen*.

The most frequent items snatched are chickens, though other small pieces of property may occasionally be claimed.[5] A sister's child does not traditionally claim his first chickens until his marriage, when he prepares a meal to terminate his wife's period of seclusion (*buwun*). He may claim as many as twenty chickens at that time, taking these both from the natal

House of his mother and that of her fictive brother. From time to time in the years thereafter he may snatch chickens as needed. Although a sister's child has claim to any of the chickens found in the courtyard of his uterine kin, he is most apt to take those of his mother's genealogical brother, or else the latter would not be "happy." There is nothing aggressive, then, about "taking things freely." If he takes a chicken from the House of his mother's fictive brother, again he may take any chicken—for all are of one House—but he should tell his mother's "brother" of his action.

Kumumen have a right which is reciprocal to that of their sisters' children. They may claim their pigs. Of the two animals, the pig is the more valuable, and so it would initially appear that the uterine kin receive the better half of the exchange. But I never gained the impression that the people think of these as reciprocal claims in this way, and the apparent inequivalence is mitigated by various factors. Chickens are claimed much more frequently than is a pig. They may be taken annually and when an individual "eats *kumumen*" (*kareng kumumen*), the entire fowl is his to consume. Pigs, on the other hand, may be claimed just once in a lifetime, for the uterine kin divide their needs among all their sisters' children. A pig is usually taken when it is needed for sacrifice and when the uterine kin themselves have none available. The meat of the animal on these occasions is always divided among all the uterine kin and a shoulder of meat is sent back to the animal's owner.

The custom of "ritual snatching" has received a great deal of attention in the ethnographic and theoretical literature on Africa. But here I focus only on the Ehing variant, which, when analyzed in its own right, provides a striking counterexample to much of the literature on this celebrated custom.[6]

One interpretation of their usage is quite simple. The people seem to conceive of the right to take things as the index of uterine connection. In that regard, people used chickens and pigs to give me a lesson on the range of kinship ties. As born by *kumumen,* sisters' children can take chickens. For the same reason, so can the children of sisters' children take fowl from the House members of their uterine grandparents. But as grandchildren are more distantly related, their rights are perceived to be those with less "force." Grandchildren take fowl less frequently. One informant used the expression that grandchildren approach "softly," like "a hunter approaching game." And with them the right ends. Their right to take chickens marks the "boundary" of *la parenté*. My informant was drawing on the resources of French to make his point because the people possess no single term which might be translated as "kinship." It is the right to "take things freely" which is the native rendering of connection. And finally, as great-grandchildren cannot take chickens, they are no longer called "children,"

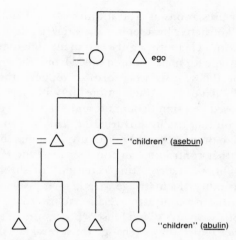

Fig. 7.3. The boundary of kinship.

but are considered *niya* (a vine), a category which also includes friends and the affines of affines.

Apart from the taking of chickens and pigs, animals figure into uterine relationships in still another way, but here only with the Houses of a mother and her fictive brother—the "possessors of the head and legs" who are the *kumumen* with whom an individual interacts most intensively. There is an affliction called "rope" (*kanie*) which attacks domestic animals, particularly cattle but also goats and pigs. When caught by "rope," an animal wobbles "as if its legs are tied together" and frequently will die. To treat "rope," an individual calls on the aid of his maternal kin who perform a ceremony called by the same name as the affliction. I did not see the ritual, but it was described to me. Two men, one from each maternal House, walk out to the pasture land to locate a small, black termite hill (*odoi*). These hills stand a foot or so high and are much smaller than the massive brown hills belonging to another species which are a more familiar part of the African landscape. The men detach the hill and attach a rope around it. The "possessor of the head" pulls the mound toward the house of his nephew or niece while the "possessor of the legs" taps it from behind as if he were driving a cow. At the house, the men dig a hole near the outside wall, pour in some water, and then bury the hill so that its "head" protrudes a little above the ground and its "feet" are buried in the earth. They then kill either a goat or pig over the hill and pray that the "other (animal)"—the cow represented by the hill—"will always be there." In this way, "rope" is treated.

There are other ritual roles defined by "possession." The "possessors of the legs" offer prestations at crucial times of transition in the lives of sisters' children. The fictive brother initially offers a gift of rice to his sister to feed her firstborn. Then other gifts "augment" the first on three occasions: a rite of passage for male children called Ichin, the initiation, and the death of a parent. These gifts are a form of support; they give "value" (*muhile,* "value," "flavor") to the relationship with her children.

That rice is used as a sign of support and value is an extension of the particular role a mother has in nurturing her children. In ritual contexts rice becomes a sign of the maternal side of production; it has this meaning even though a father contributes an equal share to the family bowl. On one other occasion, the hair cutting ceremony of the firstborn which celebrates the fecundity of a marriage, rice again is associated with maternal kin, and this time in a contrastive relation to paternal wine. During the ritual, the men of a woman's own House, "possessors of the head," bring two baskets of rice which they exchange for several jars of wine contributed by members of the father's group. These substances, wine and rice, represent the two sides that have conjoined to produce the child and the complementary labors of men and women that underlie the marriage.

And finally, in a less mystical vein, *kumumen* also offer material and political support. An individual who is short of land looks first to his uterine kin, and especially to the genealogical brothers of his mother. Though *kumumen* are under no jural obligation to lend land to their male "children" (daughters, we shall see, normatively receive land from their mothers), there is a moral expectation that they should help out if land is available. I have already cited one example in which an individual borrowed close to a hectare of paddy land. *Kumumen* also offer support and protection in political contexts. They will speak up on behalf of their children, and, in the days when certain disputes were settled by an ordeal of poison, individuals, after swallowing the poison, would await the results of the judgment with their uterine relatives. If their "child" survived, *kumumen* would sing out in celebration of the fact that he was in the right, or, in other cases, that he had been shown not to be a "witch" (*ata*). A sister's child, in turn, helps settle disputes among his *kumumen;* as a relative who is not a member of their House, he is considered an interested and yet impartial observer.

These, then, are the major ritual and social features of relations with *kumumen.* Rodney Needham (1980: 85) has remarked that, in systems of lineal descent, jural control is often balanced by mystical influence[7]; in a patrilineal context, uterine kin will be a source of physical and spiritual welfare. Taking this cue, we might say *kumumen* "possess" children since they are responsible for them: their role as producers is emphasized throughout their children's lives. At important moments of transition, they give rice; at marriages, they offer fowl; they assure the health of animals. The "children" are made of *kumumen*'s blood and are nourished with the milk of their sisters. All this is subsumed under the notion of "birth."

Understood in this sense, the ideas which define *kumumen* stand in a contrastive but complementary relation to those which connote House membership. It is possible to see these ideas as part of a pervasive social and symbolic classification in which paternal kinship contrasts with uterine, residence with possession, lineage rights with mystical influences, and wine with rice. Central to this classification, of course, are the terms male and female, for their complementarity and opposition are foundational to all the others, the fundamental part of Odieng's work.

8

Women and Land

In the banter about birth and the initiation that prefaces Part III of this study, a man and woman each seem to be vying for the last laugh. And it happens that the last retort belongs to the woman, who mocks how the initiates must leave the forest "softly"—an allusion to the central act of the rite, the cutting, that tempers the bold postures of the youth before they entered to "wrestle the heron." But whatever the outcome of the verbal competition, the larger issue is how the banter implies a contest of powers between men and women, sexual powers represented in Kombutsu and in giving birth.

When I analyzed the initiation, I suggested that Odieng's rule that excludes women is part of a conceptualization and proclamation of male rights. The same meaning, I now suggest, can be placed on the parallel rule that separates men from birth. Odieng's cloth that hides birth from men is a communication of the autonomy and necessity of female powers. The spirit, in sum, defines a duality of powers, and this duality is what the Ehing express in the banter.

In the last chapter, I began to explore the meaning and place of feminine power in social life by detailing some of the roles and contributions of women. Their contribution is rooted in the economy, but it extends, with rice as the symbol of this extension, into various social and ritual practices. In this chapter, I further explore the theme of feminine power by taking up the practices of land tenure. These practices, as I have suggested, involve an allocation of land that is—in view of all the ideas that link men, souls, and locality—strikingly anomalous. I now try to resolve this anomaly.

Intensive Agriculture, Inheritance, and Souls

Before I detail the practices that regulate the allocation of land, I want to preface the problem of women's rights by describing certain features about land, and its connection to souls, that I did not develop in my earlier discussion of the House and of the notion that "Kahin and land are one."

Most of the plains surrounding the Ehing plateau have long been converted into paddy fields; year after year people return to the same plots. New plots of land are created infrequently, and there appears little need now to do so. To say this is certainly not to deny that individuals may, at various times in their lives, lack adequate paddy, but these imbalances are most often remedied through borrowing from those who have more land than they need or want to cultivate rather than by opening new terrain.

The people are greatly attached to their paddy fields, and, although land at the present time seems adequate for the total population, in no sense is it a free good. Ehing will never alienate rice fields, and, whenever individuals loan land (a frequent practice especially among uterine relatives), they one day expect its return, whether that takes several years or a decade. The attitude toward land is readily seen in the course of disputes over claims. Sometimes these disputes involve large areas in which there is a clear and substantial economic value at stake. On other occasions, the immediate utility seems more obscure. In one case I witnessed during a public judgment, a woman insisted on reclaiming a piece of land her grandfather had loaned which must have measured no more than a few square meters. In another case, a man who had more land than he could use protected a fallow area by threatening his "brother" with a machete. Many other episodes might be cited. According to elders, their history is full of contentions and armed conflicts over rice fields. But these would add little to the general point. Living close to the people as they work their land makes it possible to glimpse a closed, contained, and jostling community, holding firm to their heritage.

This kind of attachment to land makes sense in a context of intensive agriculture, where the land embodies past labor. But, in this case, the value of land is not only economic. Land, as we have seen, is not just a resource for rice production. It is also a vehicle of reproduction, the source of souls. It is this sense of land Ehing have in mind when they say the "land and Kahin are one." And it is this sense of land they communicate in rituals at the Kahin, especially when they gather at Ihin, the harvest ritual I described in Chapter 3. Then elders celebrate the harvest with the statement that the wives of the House "should go home with an *agun* (soul)." The land gives forth both rice and children. Because land contains souls, it is indivisible from the House and the source of its perpetuity.

From an external and theoretical point of view, it is possible to take the analysis of the Kahin and souls one step further. In the context of an intensive system, it is possible to see the doctrine of souls as an idiom that primarily functions to codify the people's attachment to their land. To put this more strongly, the specific characteristics of Ehing land rights and use seem to be paralleled in the notions of souls: as the plots are fixed and enduring, so are the souls of a House, souls whose source is the fields. The same plots and the same souls cycle through the generations.

The connection between intensive agriculture and souls becomes even more striking when we recall the evidence Ehing bring to bear to point out their notion of reincarnation. The stories they tell refer to items of lost or contested property: a hatchet, a log, a stool. Now the property Ehing care most about, and the property that is the focus of the most serious and intense disputes, the only real property, is land. It is knowledge of plots that counts, knowledge of their location and their boundaries. With no deeds and with thousands of plots—large and small in village fields and in the fields of different villages—this knowledge is a fundamental legacy. And the knowledge of these scattered plots can be seen to be represented in the idea of souls. After all, they would not have forgotten the location of the fields they have already worked.

Still, in making these points, I do not want to argue that the notion of souls is nothing but an epiphenomenon of group structure and ecological relations. The global direction of my interpretation is precisely the opposite: it is that cosmological ideas and social or economic relations are not readily separable categories. The lesson in this case is that the notions of souls in part give meaning to economic activity, just as economic activity underwrites the notions of souls. I do not argue here for the priority either of symbolic classification or of economic interpretation; to set either priority would distort the very conceptions I am trying to analyze.

The Allocation of Land

It is impossible today to reconstruct the complex history of labor that has gone into the thousands of bounded plots of land that surround the

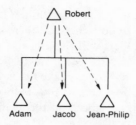

Fig. 8.1. Transmission of land from father to sons: "splitting" the fields.

villages.[1] But informants recognize that at periods in the past, as land was transmitted to meet the demands of the population, new terrain was cleared and new plots were constructed. They contrast this past labor with their own experiences in the fields, which does not generally involve the clearing of new plots but rather the annual repair of plots already in place. At some point, in other words, the transmission of land from one generation to the next occurred through the redistribution of plots rather than through the carving out of new paddy.

Contemporary transmissions of rights take place from parents to children. As a child seriously begins to contribute labor in the fields, at about the age of twelve, he or she receives a few plots of land from his or her father. The area involved in this childhood allocation (called *bala*) may measure only between 200 and 500 square meters. Both parents continue to work these plots with their child, but the rice that the mother harvests goes to the child rather than into a parental granary. This rice is used by the child in various gatherings throughout his childhood and adolescence.

The major division of the fields occurs several years after the marriage of the oldest son in a family. This division is called *bushieli,* a term which connotes splitting up an object into equal parts. In December, and before the harvest, the father, accompanied usually by his sister or another elder, out-married female agnate, walks out to his fields and places markers on the plots that are to become the boundaries of paddy land for all of his children. His sister walks along the bunds that mark these boundaries and takes some rice stalks from each side of the boundaries, taking the paddy home.

Each child will claim this paddy land as he or she comes of age and marries. But the actual dynamics of allocation within the family are somewhat more complicated, as I illustrate in Figure 8.1, using the French names of the family of a good friend. When the father, Robert, allocates his fields and gives possession of some of them to Adam, Adam will take his younger brother, Jean-Philip, into his house and feed him. Adam "raises" or fosters his younger brother; in consequence, Robert allocates to Adam several plots of land that will eventually belong to Jean-Philip.

Robert retains the use of the rest of Jean-Philip's land until he is grown and until he establishes his own household. Robert keeps his other son Jacob with him in his house. Robert will also one day take Adam's oldest child into his own house and help to feed him. Robert, in other words, will foster his oldest grandchild. He may take in, as well, the first born of his other sons to reciprocate for their having helped to feed their brothers, and perhaps as well for their labors on their father's land.

This pattern holds for all, except for a man's youngest son. Ehing practice a form of ultimogeniture. A man's youngest son tends to work with his father throughout his life, though the crop from separated fields goes into different granaries. When his father dies, and after the ritual of Kazo Odieng, the youngest claims the fields in his original allocation and the fields that the father had kept for himself. The younger son also has the right to inherit his father's house.

In any family, the process of splitting the fields is governed by the spirit called Echin. This is the same spirit that I have discussed already, in the context of the initiation, where it is the focus of an important rite of passage. Echin is a power that attacks children, bringing coughing or swollen limbs, when parents or co-wives have disputes over rice. Several weeks after splitting the fields, the family goes to the spirit's shrine to confirm the allocation, where they hope also to ensure that all parties feel the allocation has been fair.

Though I have observed rituals at Echin, I did not observe the ritual after the splitting of the fields. I was told that a father speaks at the shrine, to this effect: that he brings his son with him and that he has provided for his son and wife now for several years. If there have been domestic problems, the father explains these as well to the spirit. The son then speaks, particularly to the issue of the allocation. He may complain that a father reserved the best lands for a younger brother, or that his father does not like his wife or that his wife and mother do not get along. Or, he may explain that all is well. The point is to air grievances before the elder in charge of the shrine, so that they may be resolved. Often the elder may make a judgment, suggesting that the allocation be changed or that the allocation is fair. However, I understand that his judgment is not binding on a father. The ritual ends with the elder telling the spirit to watch over the house and to protect its inhabitants from witchcraft.

Echin is only performed as a part of traditional practice for the first born, at the original splitting of the plots. Other sons do not normally visit the shrine when they construct their own houses and take over their own fields. The other sons will visit the spirit only if Echin "catches" one of their children, and especially if a child becomes sick when there is rancor between the adults. Although fathers should divide their land

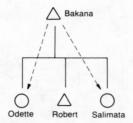

Fig. 8.2. Transmission of land from father to daughters.

equally, this is not always the case. Sometimes, the same number of paddy rows is given to each child, but the quality of land differs. Sometimes, more blatantly, the acreage is not distributed proportionately. Then sons may feel ill-will and jealousy, and, if their children should become sick in this context, the illness is likely to be interpreted as the activity of Echin. Going to the shrine, father and son air the dispute under the auspices of the spirit and the elder who administers to it.

I now turn to the transmission of rights to women. Again, I illustrate the transmission by following the allocation of a particular case (see Fig. 8.2). Like her brothers, a girl receives a few plots of land as a youngster, when she begins to help out in the fields. Her parents will do the work, but the child can keep the produce. When she marries, her father will give her several more rows of plots. In this case, Salimata receives plots of land from her father, Bakana. Salimata retains rights to this land throughout her life. And she holds rights of allocation as well as use. For she passes part of this land she received from her father to her own daughter, Marie (see Fig. 8.3). Salimata gives at least one row of plots to Marie when the latter is twelve (when Marie also receives land from her father), and Salimata may give more when Marie marries, though this is not an obligation. (Any woman, then, holds rights to land given to her from her father and her mother.)

In the context of this practice, one can better understand one form of marriage I mentioned earlier: marriage to the father's sister's daughter, called "righting the bed." A woman sends back a daughter to marry into her natal lineage, to return the seed, to produce children for that lineage. In this return, also, the land that a woman gives her daughter benefits a member of the natal lineage immediately. Pointing this out to me, my informants explained that, with this form of marriage, "the rice field doesn't move."

The intricacies of the system are revealed when Salimata dies (see Fig. 8.4). Immediately after her death, her husband may continue to cultivate the land she brought to the marriage, but her family is no longer entitled

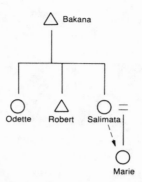

Fig. 8.3. Transmission of land from mother to daughter.

to eat any crop from her fields. Any further grain is placed in the deceased's granary, some to be used for her funeral and the remainder to be taken by the woman's daughters. The crop is expressly denied to the deceased's husband or sons.

After the final mortuary ritual, when the woman's soul has been sent back to the rice fields of her lineage, her husband is no longer permitted to cultivate her land. Part of her paddy is claimed by her sisters. Again, to follow these events in terms of a particular case, Odette informs Salimata's husband that he is no longer to cultivate the plots. But Odette's major role is to instruct her own brother, Robert, that the land is now available to be reclaimed. Odette states, in effect, to Robert that she has retaken the paddy fields of Salimata in order that they be given to Janet, Robert's daughter. As the land is reclaimed by elder women of the lineage that is its original source and passed to younger women of that same lineage, this reallocation is known as "inheriting from the father's sister" (see Fig. 8.4).

But at the same time that a sister passes land to a younger female in her lineage, Odette also offers some of the plots to her dead sister's daughter, Marie. This land, therefore, augments the plots that Salimata herself had offered to her child. This offer of additional land is especially likely to be made if Marie is married, for then the land could be well used to help support her family.

A woman, Marie, holds rights to land gained through her mother throughout her life, but at her death it is finally reclaimed by members of her mother's family. A daughter, normatively, cannot pass on rights to land transmitted to her by her mother. The land a woman gives to her own daughter is land that she herself received from her father (see Fig. 8.5).

The rules clearly are complicated and atypical of Africa and, especially, of patrilineal systems. And they seem doubly odd when viewed

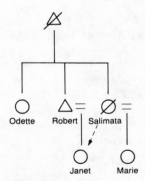

Fig. 8.4. Inheriting from "father's sister."

against the indigenous symbolic expressions and normative structures of land as the corporate property of the House. Why do women receive these rights? Why do the people go through the complicated procedure of giving land outside the lineage and then taking it back?

Before I try to answer these questions, I want to make three remarks about what I have described. First, as complicated as these rules may appear, the actual distribution of land is open to even more varied circumstances. Individuals may come into possession of plots in multiple ways. Men with many children may, for example, borrow holdings from their maternal kin. A friend inherited land from his mother's mother, at the grandmother's personal request. (I believe her lineage had suffered a decline in population and therefore had land to spare.) People in need of cattle for a sacrifice may pledge land for the animal. An old man who drinks wine continuously at the house of a relative may be expected to offer a plot in return. The point is this: in a context where there are so

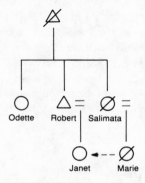

Fig. 8.5. Return of land to original House.

many plots, and with these plots scattered throughout the villages, and with the vicissitudes of experience and deaths, the system of rules "leaks" (to borrow a phrase from linguistics).

The second remark I want to make concerns the amount of land controlled by individuals. In general, men hold more land than women, and the land that they hold tends to be the more productive fields. My estimate of land held by men varies between 0.4 and 1.5 hectares. Although in most cases elders hold the larger amounts of land, occasionally their holdings are small because they already have passed many of their fields to their children. Typically, the land allotted to women is less than that held by men and may measure up to 0.3 hectare. The land given to women and passed from women to women through the generations is often the higher fields, which are more sandy and hold less water. But having made this general point, I also want to note that there are exceptions to the allocation along sexual lines. There are women in Ehing society with extensive holdings, and with more holdings than some men. A man with few or no sons will give a great amount of land to his daughters; women survivors in lineages with few or no adult men also control vast holdings. What women cannot control are the Kahin shrines that mark groups' estates in land, but the property itself is their own resource and is not merely a token.

Third, I want to point out that the rules of tenure allow the possibility that a House might lose some of its land. The rules do provoke disputes. When the current population of a House is small and when its members possess rights to more land than they can possibly cultivate, they may not reclaim the land immediately at the death of a female agnate's child. They may, that is, allow the children of their sister's children (*abulin*) to work the land. Ehing recognize the potential problem in this situation. They realize that, in allowing the grandchildren of a lineage rights to land, the land itself may become subject to dispute. It might be "lost" to the original lineage. As time passes, a grandchild might conveniently forget its original source; many of the land disputes I have recorded arise precisely out of the land gained through female connections. The point I want to stress is that dowry, as practiced by the Ehing, involves a real risk that plots may pass outside the lineage on a permanent basis and that, for Ehing, the point of the practice clearly outweighs that risk.

Explanations

How, then, are Ehing rules of land tenure to be understood? There may well be multiple determinations, both functional and historical. One way to discuss the problem is to talk directly in terms of rights. A useful and venerable distinction can be made between political rights and usufruct rights to property. In this case, it can be said that the lineage holds political rights to land—rights to ultimate allocation as well as use—and that these rights are exercised by men as the transmitters of lineage membership. As members of the lineage, women also have rights to land, but these are rights of use, since women themselves do not transmit rights to group membership. This distinction of rights is a language familiar to classic models of the British School where descent groups are seen as a basic method of allocating rights to resources.

Certainly, this depiction of rights seems to follow from the Ehing ideology of how land was first claimed and how the Kahin were used to mark the connection between the formation of groups and estates. At first glance, the rights held by women could be seen to be based on their role as "sisters," that is, as members of their lineage. Moreover, the rights in land of lineage "sisters" correspond to the other important tasks a woman takes in lineage affairs: to roles in brothers' marriage ritual and the ritual that surrounds the births of their children; in funerals; and in the division of a rice field.[2]

But still, even if women might be construed to gain rights to land as "sisters," by virtue of their active membership in their own Houses, the central question remains unanswered: how can we account for all of the rights held by women? If some women hold rights as members of the lineage, do women transfer these rights to daughters because these daughters hold residual or secondary or shadowy rights in their mother's paternal group? Is the Ehing case like that of the Tallensi, who say that since it is not women's fault they were born as women and not men, they and their children are not to be completely denied rights in their group's heritage (Fortes 1945: 149)?

In descriptive terms, this depiction of rights is unassailable. Still, I would suggest that a description of political, usufruct, or residual rights does not focus directly on specific features that define the rules of Ehing practice. Note that it is the daughters of women, and not their sons, who gain rights in land. We need to account for the specific female to female transmission, a specificity elaborated by the idiom of "inheriting from the father's sister." The mode of transmission—and the idiom that emphasizes a female control of land, a passing of rights from women to women—are not captured clearly enough in the political/usufruct contrast. In some ways, the jural explanation seems to miss the point of much of what is going on.

A second sort of interpretation might refer to ecology and adaptation. Certainly, the fact that women receive land is adaptive. In the monocultural setting of the Ehing economy, where so much depends on one staple, it is useful that a family's fields be set apart. A wide distribution of fields lowers risk. A disease that strikes a husband's fields may leave a wife's fields untouched. Rain, falling in the vicissitudes of a monsoon climate, is unevenly distributed. It makes sense, then, to hold rights to fields in different locations.

I do not want to deny the adaptive feature of land holdings. But I do want to point out that the spreading of risk is not dependent solely on the allocation of land to women. The fields of all the men are spread apart. Though a man holds the majority of his paddy fields in his residential village, these are found in different locations in the village's field. And more decidedly, a man holds rights to land in several other villages as well. Thus, the reduction of risk does not depend on women's land in an absolute sense, though it can be argued, of course, that women's land furthers the process.

A much more general application of ecology, and one that proves more helpful, is based on a contrast between intensive and extensive forms of farming. In his study of the Kofyar of Nigeria, who, like Ehing, also practice intensive agriculture, Robert Netting draws a comparison between societies where important rights to land inhere in individuals rather than in groups. Netting (1968: 159) elaborates that the Kofyar differ

> from most traditional African societies, which assign land to the collective ownership of kin groups or to a chief acting as representative of a village. . . . Typically, the individual farmer has rights of usufruct only. Such a system is a realistic and flexible adaptation to shifting cultivation, setting up as it does a pool of land from which individuals may draw according to their need and in which fallow land is held for future exploitation. Labor put into farming produces food, but it results in at least temporary loss of value in the land per se. A member of the community has rights to the products of his labor and to the necessary land on which to farm. Rights to a particular plot, however, are often lost by abandonment or terminated by death.

Netting (1968: 159) argues that intensive labor pressures a shift from land rights that are held communally to land rights that are more individuated:

> The Kofyar insist that every square inch of arable soil, both village and bush, has an owner, a single person to whom the land belongs and who alone may decide on its use. This is probably a direct outgrowth of intensive farming. Whenever land can be made to produce heavily and continuously over a long period of time, it increases in value to both the occupant and his heirs. Unlike the return

of worked-out land to the village pool, good developed homestead farmland cannot be turned over to others or to collective ownership without economic loss by the current user and windfall gain to the new possesser.

Like the Kofyar, Ehing seem to have a complex mixture of rights, some represented and held collectively, others (and perhaps the majority) held by individuals. But among the Kofyar, all these rights in land are held by men. Nonetheless, I think that Netting provides an important clue to an understanding of Ehing practice by focusing on labor as determinative of forms of rights. But where Netting sees labor in terms of costs and margins, I think it must be understood more as a substantive category—that is, in terms of its indigenous cultural meaning.

Rights and the Division of Labor

When I pressed informants for an explanation of their land practices, they always came up with the same reply. Women receive land, they say, so they can feed their husband and children for half the year. This is a simple statement, but it offers, I will argue, the solution to the problem.

Although husband and wife perform complementary labors on each other's land, the crop, we will recall, is kept strictly separate. And for half the year, rice from a woman's land goes into the family bowl, and for the rest of the year the husband's crop is eaten. What my informants explained is literally true. Women do provide rice for the family, and if not in equal amounts to men (except in polygynous households), their role as providers is nonetheless fundamental.

Now, women's rice has other uses as well. We have seen that a mother has special responsibility for feeding infants; for the first year or so, a child will only eat mother's rice. And rice figures into ritual, where there is an association of rice with women in contrast to an association of wine with men. When women speak at funerals, they offer gifts of rice to the deceased; men offer gifts of wine. In various rites of passage, women offer their children rice, or uterine kin offer rice to these children in contrast to paternal kin who offer wine. This offering occurs in the hair-cutting ceremony, at Echin, and during the initiation. Only women bring rice when they visit Odieng, where it stands as a symbol of their labor in contrast to the wine provided by men. Rice, furthermore, signifies a connection between women in their labor—the rice of a granary passes from mothers to daughters. Rice, which is transplanted and harvested by women, is, in short, a symbol of female productive capacities and roles.

My argument here is that the rights in land held by women directly reflect this female productive capacity. In other words, the rights are founded on the necessary and fundamental contributions of women in producing rice, in creating children, and in feeding children. In saying this, I do not rest my interpretation on any general theory that rights rest on contributions of labor, for in many societies the value of women's labor is unrecognized and labor may be subject to different forms of alienation. But for Ehing, the work of women is highly valued. In addition, women control not only their own labor in farming but also the products of much of their work as well. The direct rights women hold in land are an integral component of this cultural construction of feminine power.

What makes the rules of tenure so complex is that the set of rights held by women stands in contradiction to the other idea that the House and land are one and that the House is conceived of as a line through men. In point of fact, then, two opposing ideas about land are operative. Because of the link between Houses and land, the land passed outside a lineage eventually is called back. But notice that, even when it is called back, it is reclaimed by women, and these women instruct their brothers to pass it to their daughters. If land, in other words, reverts to the lineage, it is land still controlled by women. In effect, rights to land are defined by notions of gender as well as, and perhaps even more than, notions of descent.

Following Netting, then, I agree that land tenure follows from forms of labor. But I argue that these forms of labor must be understood in terms of indigenous meanings. In the Ehing case, the division of labor is conveyed in terms that "men build houses" and "women give birth." And it is as part of this construction of gender and labor that rice images the powers of women and that women use their land, as the people told me, to feed their children.

9

The Absent King

Of all the rules governed by Odieng, two initially struck me as the most inscrutable: the prohibitions on seeing the "king" eat and on mixing palm wine and water. In comparison with the rules I have already discussed, these seemed somehow out of place. Sexuality, death, and initiation intuitively seemed connected, or at least connectable in many ways; but what did these have in common with wine and water, or the "king"? Almost as a way of wishing the problem away, I checked and rechecked that these rules indeed were the work of Odieng. They are; and I will show in this chapter that the two rules are linked to Odieng by an internal association.

The interpretive problem of making sense of these rules is one that is compounded by the curious office of the kingship. It seems that the "king" is a figure who is absent as much as he is present. And so, for at least half a century the people have not had to worry about violating the "king's" rule of the Hatchet.

The word I have translated as "king" is *ai,* which is cognate with the Diola *oei*. The translation is misleading and must be given a particular meaning. But it is the translation used by those Ehing who speak French. "King" is misleading because the *ai* is more a ritual than a political figure, and because the society can hardly be said to constitute a kingdom. On the contrary, there is no system of indigenous political offices, and the *ai* is not even a figurehead in any political system. The office of village chief was introduced by the French for administrative reasons, primarily tax collection, and today chiefs have no political power. The acephalous character of Casamance groups—including those Diola groups south of the river who likewise have an *oei*—stands in sharp contrast to other polities in the surrounding area, especially to the stratified kingdom of the Manjaco just south of the Ehing.

There has not been a living king among the Ehing since Kuputi, the last incumbent, died some sixty years ago. Because the living elders of his House were then too young to be privy to the mysteries of his office, the information they were able to provide is fragmentary. They recounted a brief and not altogether consistent history of the institution. The first king among them, Akula, was an immigrant and, by legend, not altogether welcome when he arrived. He is said to have come from either the village of Karuhai or Bubul, both of which are now located in Guinea-Bissau. Akula arrived first in the village of Nyame, and there various families took up the question of his permanent residence. The Bassene families of Nyame suggested that a family of Sagna take him in, but the Sagna apparently refused. Thereafter, Akula was led to House Naligera at Bakunum, and, after convoking the other Bassene of Ehing society, Naligera decided to give him land and he started a House. Akula brought with him various ritual paraphernalia associated with his office: a red cloth and hat, a special gourd (called *asundu*), a yellow disclike object, and two bars of iron.

The gourd, disc, and pieces of iron are stored in a small hut across from Kuputi's crumbled house. Once a year or so, the elders of Kula perform a libation within, but they never allowed me to enter the hut to view the royal objects.

The iron that the *ai* brought with him is especially interesting because the Bassene, who eventually accepted the king, were the traditional blacksmiths of Ehing society. Perhaps, then, it is no coincidence that the Sagna clan rejected him. Although the Bassene no longer practice forging, they are presently responsible for a spirit called Teno (fire), which burns houses and causes leprosy. No one remembers whether this spirit existed before the king's arrival, but in all probability the kingship is an institution which was actively integrated into, and modified to fit, an already complex system of ritual symbolism.

Since Akula's arrival, there have been at least six other *ai*. Ehing do not keep any formal genealogy of names, and to gather the list of six I had to visit several of the elders of House Kula, each of whom only gave a few names. Furthermore, none of the present-day elders recall anything more than fragments of Kuputi's inauguration, since the only three who were then alive were only children. Ehing apparently feel that, when they are next ready for a king, they will be able to recruit persons from the south to come and direct the ritual by which he is installed.

How is an *ai* chosen? According to tradition, or at least the "tradition" which is now recounted by elders, the office of *ai* does not pass immediately from one person to the next. Instead, the selection of an *ai,* though limited to a member of House Kula in the village of Bakunum (patronym Bassene), must await the appearance of certain signs that foretell the successor to the office. One sign is that Ehing will recognize a new *ai* when a child of Kula does not become wet while out in the rain. The other is that, when the child is given water, it will change to wine and, when given wine, it will change into water. Thus, this power to transform wine and water places these substances, through the person of the *ai,* into a kind of contact that seems analogous to the real act of mixing these substances which Odieng forbids among normal persons. Here is the connection between the two interdictions.

Apart from the signs I have already mentioned, there is another rule which governs selection to office. No one can become an *ai* who was himself living while the previous *ai* reigned. In terms of this requirement, House Kula is now in its second generation of potential candidates, and I repeatedly heard stories of one person or another having shown the signs. These stories were always denied by the individuals themselves. One person, for example, pointed out that he is left-handed. Since the *ai* must be right-handed, he could not have remained dry in the rain as had been rumored. His brother added that an individual selected by the signs could not deny them or deny the assumption to office. Nevertheless, Ehing do say that it is "hard" to become *ai* and it is not an office which seems to be sought. I was told unverifiable stories of a father, who, when he saw his child dry, ran and fetched a container of water to wet the child. At one time I attributed these and other statements of reluctance to a diffuse hesitancy among Ehing openly to seek positions of authority over others. While I still believe in this characteristic, I learned later of another belief which offers a more specific reason why the kingship is "hard." The elders of Kula told me that an *ai* cannot be installed while his parents are alive. I was told that to meet this requirement the entire assembly of Bassene might have to be convoked to kill the parents by supernatural means. It is hard to know how literally one is to take this kind of statement—is it a fiction, or were parents actually poisoned? There is a symmetry here between this belief and that about the *ai*'s successor, in that neither parents or successor can see the *ai* in office. Once the parents of the prospective *ai* were dead, the candidate himself would one day be seized by the House of

Buzenu (Sagna, Bakunum); in this way, against the protests of the House of Kula, the preparations for his installation would begin.

Before installation, the *ai* would live for a year in a hut at Nyame, near the grand Odieng, while his house was being built at Bakunum. He was joined there by his first wife, who was always a woman from the village of Etafun.[1] After this year of social invisibility, the *ai* was taken while sitting on a cow, which had not yet ever calved, to the patch of forest in Bakunum's rice fields, where the ceremonies of Kombutsu are also conducted. There, he was given a new name and also participated in what were apparently elaborate ceremonies which no Ehing now remembers. Afterward, the *ai* was escorted to his new house accompanied by his wife, who by this time should have become pregnant. The house of the *ai* was said to have been slightly larger than other Ehing houses, with many sleeping rooms, and in the course of his life the *ai* was expected to take a wife for each room. An *ai* need not offer wine for a wife like other Ehing; instead a woman would simply be taken without any compensation for her. She was "caught," so the description goes, by attaching a bracelet of iron to her wrist. According to my informants, the parents of a woman were quite unhappy when she was chosen to be the *ai*'s wife. The last *ai* at one time had five wives. He later divorced one of these, and no other Ehing was permitted to marry her.

The *ai* performed both ritual and political duties. The ritual duties of the *ai* centered on his ability to produce rain and in this way safeguard the prosperity of his people; better than "king," *ai* might be translated as "rain-priest." Especially in times of drought, the *ai* would offer the souls of black animals (bulls, pigs, chickens) to his spirit, Kai, and was entitled to claim any animals needed for this purpose without giving their owners any compensation. Ehing also said that the *ai* was able to take the souls of these animals to Iri, in the eastern sky, the direction from which the rains arrive. If the *ai* "didn't do his work well," the people would chase him from office.

What political power the *ai* could exercise probably derived from his ritual role. He is said to have had the power to adjudicate particularly chronic or disruptive disputes over land; when the parties would not abide by his decision, he could confiscate the land in question. I do not know by what actual means confiscation was accomplished. I was told that he placed a stick to mark the boundaries of the contested plots, but what was the source of his authority? The people never spoke of any sort of identification between *ai* and land, which is a common feature of sacred kings in Africa; the *ai* was not a "master of the earth."[2] His line was itself a line of immigrants with no first, original claims. And he apparently had no physical force at his disposal. What he did have, however, was control over his spirit Kai, and hence control of the rains. He might have used this as a form of power.

As the owner of lands, the *ai* was expected to provide fields to any immigrant who came to settle permanently among the Ehing. But, although he owned land, the *ai* himself was prohibited from performing any work. During the rainy season, he was not even allowed to enter the fields; if he were to do so, he would kill the growing rice and set the fields themselves ablaze.[3] His fields were cultivated by Ehing youth and members of the Bassene clan. The rice gained was stored in a special granary and would be used to supply needy families if they ran out of rice. In return, those who had received rice would give the *ai* wine during the dry season, for he was also not allowed to tap palms. I was told that the last king died because he broke the prohibition on work when he felled a tree.

During the season of darkened skies, when the *ai* promoted rain, he wore only black clothes. But during the dry season, he donned his red clothes, the color Akula wore when he first arrived among the Ehing. It is also, as one of my informants said, the color associated with Kombutsu and a color that points to the many ways the figure of the *ai* is associated with fire.

The *ai* is represented as a source of fire, as I have said, in that he had the power to ignite the rice fields. His identification with fire is also conveyed in his funeral ceremonies. Like many sacred figures throughout Africa, the *ai* is not ever said to "die" but to be "lost." His body was buried secretly at Nyame by members of his House, but they made no public announcement until a year later when a special dance called *ekoi* was held. During this event, described to me as a spectacular affair which lasted a week, the elder of Odieng clanged the *ai*'s pieces of iron and the sisters of the *ai* carried his special gourd with a cow's heart placed in it. At the end of the week, the members of the *ai*'s family performed a ceremony called Kaditsen Teno, "Tossing Water On the Fire." An elder collected the vine of a highly abrasive plant called *teno* ("fire"), ground up the vine, and placed it in a bowl of wine. Water was then added to the mixture, which "extinguished" the fire, and the elder tossed droplets of the mixture onto the people at the *ai*'s dance. Any persons who were at part of the dance and did not return for this ceremony would find that their houses would burn down. "Tossing Water On the Fire" was also performed in lieu of the ritual of separation (Kazo Odieng) for the kin of the deceased *ai*. As the "king" is fiery, to end contact with him Ehing symbolically doused themselves. The whole notion of the *ai*'s association with fire may now be seen to have been prefigured by the sign that as a child he did not become wet.

The House of Kula, the House of the *ai,* is connected with fire in other ways. Before covering a house with straw all Ehing must go libate at the Kahin of that House: "It is the custom when covering a house to come here. I want to stay in the house in peace. Even if a fire escapes (the hearth), it cannot do anything. And even if there is a bush fire, the wind will blow in the other direction." If the libation is not performed, the spirit "Fire" (Teno), whose shrine is delegated to House Kula, will ignite the house. Houses burn, of course, in spite of this libation—lightning, accidents, brush fires all take their toll. When this occurs, it is the responsibility of House Kula to perform "Tossing Water On the Fire" on the remains of the house and on its former occupants.

House Kula, finally, is associated with fire by way of leprosy. Ehing call this disease the "terrible sickness" and sometimes the "terrible fire," and its onset is associated with the spirit Teno for whom Kula are responsible. A leper was isolated in a hut in the bush and cared for by members of Kula, who are thought immune to the disease. If the ill individual should die, House Kula buried him without ceremony and thereafter performed the ritual of "Tossing Water On the Fire" on the hut where the leper had lived, on his surviving kin, and on themselves. Ehing further said that the marriage of an incipient leper to a member of Kula would stop any further development of the disease.[4]

This is the information given to me about the institution of the *ai*. The details are sparse, and it is difficult to reach any firm conclusions about the position of the *ai* in Ehing cosmology. As I noted, a similar figure is found among various Diola groups throughout the Casamance and in Guinea-Bissau; furthermore, many features of the Ehing *ai* are common in other areas of Africa. Many high priests or sacred kings, for example, are thought to control the rains, and the prohibition on seeing them eat is common also. As conveyers of ecological and often cosmic order, it is hardly surprising that such figures are set apart.

For the Ehing, it certainly seems that the idea of *ai* is just as significant as any performance of duty by an actual incumbent. Elders of House Kula can still libate at the Kai in his absence to ask for *mazunemi* (well-being) and rain; and in the 1940s the people imported a Diola spirit called Kasora which they supplicate in times of drought. Then, too, the limited juridical functions have been replaced by the ability to take land disputes to representatives of the Senegalese government. Most importantly, if one were to take at face value the beliefs of the *ai*'s incarnation, the office was almost vacant as much as it was filled. This is not an Ashanti kingship, nor even a figure who promoted political integration as does the Shilluk divine king who, in Evans-Pritchard's characterization, "reigns but does not govern" (1962: 74).

What place, then, does the *ai* hold in ideology? What is his cosmological meaning? We might gain an answer by piecing together his attributes. The *ai* is a source of fire and yet also a "master" of water: his colors are red and black. This duality of function and of color parallels the duality of the seasons—the rains and the heat—and this parallel is coded through the very signs which foretell the person who will hold the office. Here lies the solution. The figure of the *ai* symbolically mediates the change of seasons: he turns wine (dry season) into water (wet season). And, as agent of this transformation of seasons, he is not allowed to identify himself with either, and he does no work. This, then, is his place in the cosmology—to ensure the natural round on which production is based.

Perhaps more obliquely, the *ai* is not only associated with the fertility of the land but also with that of persons—a notion intimated by his taking of many wives and by the pregnancy of his first. In that he cannot be caught by Odieng, he also might have been thought, like the spirit, to mediate between men and women, though this notion remains undeveloped.

What is more clear is that the association of *ai* and Odieng builds up the analogy between the duality of the sexes and the duality of the seasons. This analogy (male is to female as the dry season is to the rainy season) has already been implied in the ritual associations of men with wine and women with rice. As the *ai* mediates the seasons, Odieng defines the relations between the sexes, and the proper relation of both is necessary for the production of land and for that of persons. And, since the *ai* is a taboo of Odieng, it is through the "king" that the spirit conceptually integrates natural and social experience.

10

The Hatchet's Fall

Odieng appears in the world not only as a source of moral rules and affliction, but also as a hatchet which falls from the sky. Odieng Iri, "hatchet of the sky," plummets to the earth, Ehing say, as a flaming piece of iron which may ignite trees and bush before disappearing into the ground. Sometimes the force is so great that a tree in the hatchet's path is completely split in two. When Odieng Iri first strikes the ground, moreover, the impact is said to render unconscious any person who is in the vicinity of its fall. The people say that if one individual, on these occasions, awakens before others, he must not call out to them lest they die.

As time passes, the hatchet which has fallen slowly moves upward through the earth until reaching the surface of the land.[1] Anyone who finds Odieng Iri may take it home, for it is associated with good fortune (*mazunemi*). Sometimes, the hatchet is buried under a Kahin. However, Odieng Iri does not fall often, and I was unable to find anyone who had a hatchet.

Any fire which Odieng Iri starts has a special meaning for Ehing. The women in the village where the hatchet strikes quench their cooking fires, sweep away all ash from their hearths, and thereupon go to obtain fire from the new source. Ehing distinguish this fire from the fire caused by lightning, which more commonly ignites bush or houses. However, both the fire of Odieng Iri and lightning are associated with the "king's" family. The lightning that strikes a house is often perceived as the manifestation of the spirit Teno (fire), which is under control of House Kula; and when Odieng Iri produces a fire in Bakunum, it is the women of Kula who are the first to gather the new fire and lead it into the village. The associations between the *ai* himself and Odieng Iri are even more direct. As both are a source of fire, each is draped in red, and the *ai* arrived carrying iron.

Strictly speaking, the spirit Odieng and Odieng Iri are not identical forms, but they are associated linguistically and conceptually, and they are not entirely distinguishable. The appearance of the spirit has also been described as "like fire": the redness of fire and blood are the two modes by which the spirit is visible. And in Ehing thought, the spirit, like Odieng Iri, also "fell" when it was first placed to do its work in Ehing society.

Odieng's Arrival

The image of Odieng's fall is found in the story that explains the spirit's introduction to society. Unlike the beliefs and practices related to Odieng Iri, which are current throughout the population, this story appears to be known only by the members of Houses responsible for the shrines. The text I present here was related by the son of a deceased priest of Nyame's shrine. Since no names are given in the story, I have replaced the constant use of pronouns, which make things confusing, with the names of Nyame and Karaguba, the sites where the two shrines are located.

> When the Ehing left Iribun, they brought the "grand Odieng" with them and placed it at the village of Kuguo. Afterward a man of House Karaguba brought Odieng from Kuguo to the place where one goes when one is sick because of doing something which is taboo. The shrines found now at Nyame and Karaguba are the same thing, but there are two because of a woman of Karaguba called Adimen who married at Nyame (*adimen* also means "out-married woman").
>
> Each time the man of Karaguba went to visit the spirit, he would greet his brother-in-law on the way to Kuguo. And each time he returned, he passed by the house of his brother-in-law who gave him wine to drink. But the day that Karaguba planned to bring back the spirit with him, he passed the house at Nyame without calling out a greeting. But his brother-in-law had seen him pass by and knew why he went to Kuguo.
>
> After his brother-in-law had gone by, the man of Nyame went to get wine and to sit near the path. The place where he was sitting is

where the shrine is now located. The moon was full. After a while, Nyame saw his brother-in-law returning. Nyame called out to him but received no answer. Instead of answering, Karaguba put the spirit in a *kalu* (container). Nyame called out again, but again Karaguba did not answer. Finally Nyame asked, "What's the matter?" Karaguba said nothing. Nyame said, "No. If you don't come here, I'll think I did something." The brother-in-law should have refused to go. Nyame had insisted until his brother-in-law came to drink.

He came and they drank the wine together. When they drank, Karaguba placed the *kalu* above (in the rafters of the roof), and they drank until Karaguba was drunk. When Nyame knew that Karaguba had drunk too much, Karaguba said, "I want to go home." Nyame said, "We'll go. I'll accompany you." After he had accompanied him part way, Nyame hurried back to the *kalu*. Arriving, he cut the *kalu* (in another recitation from the same informant, he cut the cord which was wrapped around the *kalu*), and Odieng fell to the ground.

Meanwhile, the man of Karaguba went to sleep. As he slept, Odieng went to find him as in a dream. The spirit said, "You told me to come live with you. Where I am (that is, at Nyame), is that where you live?" The man woke up and went out into the night, going back to his brother-in-law's.

He said, "I had something; it is lost." (Alternatively, "I had something which I forgot.") Nyame responded, "But when we were sitting here, you said nothing to me. I don't know if you had something with you. What you forgot, where did you put it?"

Nyame felt over the ground to search for the *kalu*. When he saw it, he looked down and saw that the sand was glowing like fire. Nyame said, "Oh! It's torn. There are many mice here. Probably the mice ripped it."

Karaguba who had brought it from Kuguo, he also looked down at the ground. He saw the spirit glowing there, and he didn't know how to reclaim it. He went home.

The next day Karaguba went again to Kuguo to seek another shrine. Odieng told him, "I told you, if you passed by the house of your brother-in-law, he would take it. The first that you took will be the more important shrine; there will be a small house there. Whenever someone sees a taboo, he will go there; if they don't go there, it's because the elder of Odieng at Nyame is dead. Since he is your brother-in-law, it's finished. It's good, you will be one House."

One key feature of the story is the social context in which Odieng is placed. The men in the story are brothers-in-law (*kuluo*), and a dominant feature of their relationship in this brief plot is a tension over possession of the spirit. The wife-giver (Karaguba) originally finds the spirit at Kuguo.[2] Returning from his visits to the shrine, Karaguba stops at Nyame to drink wine. Offering wine to a brother-in-law is a typical and frequent occurrence, which continues the prestations of wine that traditionally precede a marriage. The behavior of Karaguba on the day he plans to bring back Odieng is also typical, if not quite proper. In Ehing etiquette, a person should always call out a greeting when passing another's house, and this is especially true among relatives by marriage. In everyday life when a greeting is not forthcoming, Ehing often suspect that the passer-by has something he does not want to share. Frequently, this something is fish. Thus, it makes sense to Ehing that, when Karaguba was silent, Nyame knew that he had something.

To hide the spirit on his return, Karaguba places it in a *kalu*. A *kalu* is a crescent-shaped container made from a fan-palm leaf. Before the introduction of bottles, these containers were attached to palm trees to gather the sap for wine. I was also told that *kalu* were traditionally used after the circumcision to catch the blood of the initiates as they went to Kahus in order to prevent it from touching the ground, where it might be seen by women; it was in a *kalu* that the bloodied leaves of the initiates were stored in the Kombutsu I described. When, in the myth, Karaguba reluctantly arrives at his brother-in-law's house, he places the *kalu* "up high," and there it is forgotten because of the wine. From an initial, if momentary, refusal to drink, Karaguba succumbs to excess, and perhaps this excess is determined by, or expresses, his inevitable loss of the spirit. Mythic plots are often teleological in this sense.

The detail of "height" is evocative; it sets up Odieng's fall. We have seen that "height" is associated with a provocation of blood loss; women during menstruation and after birth, and male initiates, are forbidden to go "up high." In the story, Odieng falls out of the *kalu* because the container is "cut" (*nasu*) by Nyame, and where the spirit falls is "like fire," is red. Now, in the context of an affinal relationship, these images of cutting, falling, bleeding, suggest nothing so much as a "delivery" and the sexuality which precedes a birth. Odieng "falls" into the house of Nyame, the wife-taker, and the path of the spirit in the story is analogous to the movement of a woman. We might recall here that Ehing denote the movement of a soul into a woman by the verb "to fall" (*kalolo*).[3]

The metaphor of birth seems to be developed as the story progresses. Odieng comes to Karaguba as he sleeps and poses a question of residence, a concept that is central to notions of reproduction. This question is answered when Karaguba discovers the shrine at Nyame's house but cannot reclaim it. Karaguba has, in some sense, lost Odieng. He must settle for another, but secondary, shrine and, on this note of resolution, the story seems to end. Although the men are of different Houses, these Houses are united as "one," perhaps as Houses are allied through the exchange of women but—more directly—as they are tied through a child who literally is created by the members of each.

Separation and Contradiction

That Odieng's arrival in the story is represented as a birth testifies to its essential role in Ehing life: as a birth marks the beginning of an individual's life, Odieng's work, conceptually, marks the origin of a particular way of life. The image points precisely to what I have argued is the meaning of the spirit's rules.

In the study of these rules, I have put special emphasis on notions of sexual separation, and my analysis has been structured by following out the implications of the text of the first marriage. Now here, in the story of Odieng's arrival, the image of birth seems to echo back to the theme with which I began. In fact, these two stories seem to be transformations of one structure. The theme in each story is a problem in residence. In the marriage tale, the problem revolves around where the man and woman are to live. In the text of Odieng's arrival, the problem concerns the location of the spirit. Each text also ends with a similar conclusion: The woman ends up moving into the man's house. The shrine ends up in the place to which a woman moves—that is, at the house of the in-law who received a wife.

In comparing the two stories on this point, it is intriguing to recall that the shrine today found at Nyame, at Sisa's house, is, in fact, the shrine enclosed in a thatched roof. It is a shrine in a house, while the other shrine located on the land of Karaguba House, like the woman's original shelter in the marriage text, is nothing but a hole in the ground.

In both texts, the problem of residence is cast in an idiom of tension and struggle. In the marriage text, the struggle is about where a woman is to give birth. At issue, as we have seen through an analysis of ideas of souls and land, is the concept of descent. Now this is the same issue that is evoked in the text of Odieng's arrival. As the placing of the shrine is evocative of birth, the tension over its possession echoes the same theme as that of the story of man and woman.

The differences in the texts, and the axis of their transformation, lie in their approximations to ordinary social experience. In the marriage tale, the tension is presented in more general terms. The terrain in the text, like that in a play by Beckett, is stark, stripped of any details of village life. The categories in the text are fundamental: man and woman, the categories of gender. And their mediation is produced through basic elements: rain and sexual desire.

In the story of Odieng's arrival, the tension is cast as that between brothers-in-law. These are actual and ordinary social roles, and roles that in the story are used to represent the relationship between lineages. Correspondingly, the tension in the text over possession of the shrine is mediated by an explicit balance: there will be two shrines, and the Houses will be united as one.

So much for the primary similarities and differences in the stories. What I want to stress here is that, in both of these stories, the issue is what, in anthropological terms, amounts to competing claims in reproductive rights. Ehing myth, as I have argued, is an indigenous theory of society; and this theory is one that tells of the complementary and antagonistic "forces" of men and women. These forces are what make claims to rights tense and ambiguous. Tension and ambiguity are inherent in Ehing notions of reproduction, and that is the repeated message in the texts.

Interestingly enough, this message is also a familiar feature in the models anthropologists themselves have developed in the study of descent. Specifically, what the Ehing say through these stories is analogous to the way in which anthropologists have explored the idea that descent involves an alienation of reproductive rights. Aidan Southall (1986: 17) puts his finger on exactly what the Ehing seem to be working on when he writes:

> Men in societies of subsistence herding and cultivating usually control more of public life and property than women do, seeing themselves as the dominant factor in society. This always brings them up against the uncomfortable fact that they cannot reproduce their society without women. This contradiction is everywhere worked out in symbol, myth, and ritual. Men seeing themselves as dominant may be extended to a wish to see their lines as dominant.

The important point here is that, for Ehing, the contradiction is both existential and social. It is existential in the sheer brute sense of the physical facts of reproduction, as these are recognized by the people. But more essentially, the contradiction arises in Ehing thought because of the cultural meaning of "giving birth." In other words, the contradiction and tension about rights arise because the rights of men are challenged by the powers and value of women. This challenge is the pivot of Ehing social thought.

Lévi-Strauss has suggested that myths can be seen as attempts to overcome, disguise, or mediate contradictions (1967: 30). Although I have regarded Ehing stories more as indigenous theory than as attempts at resolving in thought what cannot be resolved in life, there are certainly attempts at mediation here as well. Evidence of this mediation can be seen in the relations between the two texts themselves. The tale of Odieng's arrival is working on the problem that is presented in starker terms in the marriage tale. The woman has dropped out of the picture, and instead of a polarity of man and woman, we have man and man. And instead of an absolute choice between residences (and the "forces" of men and women these residences symbolize), we have the spirit represented at two shrines. The opposition in the texts becomes less intense as the frame of reference moves from the world of myth to that of social life.

The Source of Odieng's Power

I began this book with a description of Odieng's power, which Ehing know as the affliction the spirit brings. My aim has been to make an interpretation of this affliction; in doing so, I have focused on how its deadly power to afflict may be taken as a symbol of its social meaning.

The placing of Odieng at the center of this study was not arbitrary. The Ehing themselves initially pointed out the role of the spirit to me. They did so in conversations when they alluded to a singular place the spirit held in their cosmos; more to the point, they did so in the graphic description of how the spirit attacks. Evans-Pritchard (1956: 313) has suggested that the best way into the philosophy of an African people is through their notions of affliction. In the Ehing case, this suggestion points to the activity of the Hatchet.

But if I have taken the direction implied in Evans-Pritchard's remark, the problems I have encountered were somewhat different. In *Nuer Religion*, Evans-Pritchard (1956: 320) "tried . . . to interpret (the religion) as a system of ideas and practices in its own right." Although some features of this religion, as Evans-Pritchard says, can be made more "intelligible" in relation to the social order, his focus was on the personal meaning of Kwoth to the Nuer. In trying to interpret Odieng, I have, in part, adopted Evans-Pritchard's method. I too have concentrated on the ideas and practices of religious categories as a logical system. But I have turned his perspective around. Ehing religious thought is directly involved with the definition of social groups and the economy (cf. Beidelman 1971), and part of what I have tried to do is to show how the social order is made more intelligible in relation to religious thought.

In adopting the position that symbols define major social principles, I join several recent writers whose work on West African social structures rests on a theory of symbolic classification, especially Jackson (1977) and Bisilliat (1983) whose work focuses on gender. One implication of these studies, and one that I have tried to develop here, is that concepts of gender and cosmology are independent of, and, in a logical sense, prior to the pattern of rights that comprise systems of descent, marriage, and property.[4] Jackson (1977: 91), for example, in his monograph on the Kuranko of Sierra Leone, points out that, although "the importance of the patriline is emphasized in the Kuranko dogma of descent, the complete elucidation of Kuranko social structure requires us to explore the complementary aspects of its implicitly bilineal character." And he relates this bilineal character of descent to a conceptual scheme, arguing that the foundations of Kuranko thought rest on how "maleness is correlated with order, life, seed, primary production, control, and the supervision of the most difficult tasks, while femaleness is correlated with secondary, nurturant, and mediatory roles" (Jackson 1977: 86).

Bisilliat also focuses on the social implications of gender, but she takes her argument in a different direction. Although she too documents a mode of classification in her work among the Songhay-Zarma (1985), she further emphasizes the incongruity between an ideology of patrilineal descent and a culturally recognized complementarity between the sexes.

Like the peoples in these studies, the Ehing offer a striking instance of ideas about sexual complementarity and contradiction. But perhaps what makes their world of particular ethnographic interest is how these ideas are conveyed though a coherent system of ritual. The point I want to make here is not only that Odieng embodies so many social meanings; Odieng has been my interpretative problem, but my larger aim has been to show in detail how an understanding of Ehing social life depends upon the analysis of ritual symbolism.

At this point I can return to my original question: what are the social sources of Odieng's power? Certainly part of Odieng's power rests on the spirit's pervasive and general role in bringing order to social experience. Through its affliction, Odieng protects a system of classification. The spirit, in this sense, is very much like other complex categories of African thought, like the Nuer concept of Kwoth, which, to call again on Douglas's apt phrase, punishes "a breaking of that which should be joined or joining of that which should be separate" (1966: 113). That Odieng provides just such a symbolic foundation is easy enough to see. It separates men from women, youth from elders, and the king from his people. Its rules make a statement about the relation between the living and the dead. It separates substances as well, in the rule of wine and water. Finally, through the figure of the "king," which shares the colors of the spirit, the order necessary for natural production—the duality of the seasons—

becomes a cosmological extension of the union and separation of the sexes. The spirit is a virtual instrument of classificatory thought.[5]

Still, I have argued that Odieng's power reflects more than its general role in defining and maintaining categories. The spirit, I have tried to show, governs production and reproduction. Through its rules of separating initiation and birth, Odieng defines a division of labor: the rules about the cover between the sexes are a way to define powers and rights, and these powers and rights are embodied in the notions of "building houses" and "giving birth."

It is in terms of this division of labor of building houses and giving birth, this conception of gender, that I have explored two problems: the tension in Ehing thought about possession of children and the anomaly in the system of land tenure. Rights in reproduction and in land are contradictory, and at this point it can be seen that the contradictions I have traced in reproductive rights and land rights are intricately related. More to the point, both contradictions are traceable to the same source—the competing "forces" of men and women. The reason that women possess land is the same reason that accounts for the tension in Ehing myths—women, necessarily and fundamentally, "give birth." And that is the message of Odieng's rule that keeps men away.

At the same time, it must be recognized that there is an asymmetry in Odieng's work. There are, after all, Houses in Ehing society, and Odieng is central to their construction. In the initiation, especially, we have seen that it is through the spirit that men appropriate a symbol of female fertility and through this symbol construct the idea of a line of souls. Through this definition of their powers, in other words, men build Houses and hold rights to children that are otherwise physically produced by women. And so, as much as the spirit might define the powers of both sexes, its rules nonetheless mediate these powers in favor of male rights. This mediation is also part of the spirit's work.

The ideas about gender defined by Odieng, then, are complex ideas, in which there are relations of symmetry and asymmetry. And the work of the spirit is yet again more complex, for its prohibitions link the powers of gender to land, to farming, even to the passing of the seasons. And it is this entire work, finally, that is the source of the spirit's own power. Odieng can take life because a way of life depends on its activity.

And with that, I have said what I can about the Hatchet. What I have tried to do is to encounter Odieng by making an interpretation of it—to show how Ehing have made a world of meaning through a blade of iron. Like any interpretation, this encounter has not exhausted the representation, and, like any interpretation, it ends with questions left open. I very much regret that I never had the chance to visit Odieng's major shrine, the shrine reserved for beginning and ending the initiation. This is not because I would not have been allowed, but because Ehing meet Odieng there only on prescribed occasions, which never occurred while I was among them. Deep in the woods, the shrine is not visible, and without a guide I would not have found my way. And more importantly, what would be there to see? A hole in the ground, perhaps under the shade of a tree, and probably overgrown with weeds. And so there is a very concrete sense in which Odieng remains opaque. But an elder once told me that when the men meet Odieng at its major shrine, when they offer it wine and sometimes blood, they are "arm and arm" with the spirit. This is an image of friendship—the deadly spirit and the people "arm and arm," as friends who walk together along a path. And perhaps it is wise to let an elder have this last word.

Reference Material

Notes to Chapters

Preface

1. The first extensive ethnographic survey of the Diola was completed by Thomas (1958/59). Other major writings on the people include those of Sapir (1970, 1977, 1981), Linares (1970, 1981), Snyder (1981), and Mark (1985).

Chapter 1: Odieng's Rules

1. For more general critiques of Douglas's argument, see Ardener (1967) and Sahlins (1976).

Chapter 2: Odieng's Ritual

1. In this range of meanings, Iri is identical to the Diola concept *Emitay*. See Sapir (1970).
2. The symptoms of Odieng's presence are described in such specific terms that one might be tempted to ask if they correspond to those of a particular disease. Perhaps the most likely candidate would be malaria, which like the sickness of Odieng, goes through a cycle of attack and remission, produces a great headache, and a fever high enough that it might be described to be "like fire." Even more intriguing is the parallel that mosquitoes, like Odieng, drink blood. But alas, the

people do not link mosquitoes with the onset of affliction; the correspondence amounts to nothing but coincidence. Even if a connection could be made, this would not imply that Odieng could be reduced to natural phenomena. It would only show how people use the world in their imaginative works.

3. When a young person comes to the spirit to confess, he often does not make his own statement. Rather, an elder accompanies him to the shrine and, from a position several yards from the shrine, speaks on behalf of the child.

4. The importance of ingesting blood is underscored by the name of a plant called "medicine of Odieng" (*bubun* Odieng). I was told that instead of going to the shrine, a person may attempt to cure himself by soaking the leaves in water and then drinking the red mixture. However, I know of no person who actually performed this operation, and I doubt whether anyone who had would mention it. The informant who told me of the plant insisted that knowledge of its existence is esoteric.

5. The structure of this ritual which I have thus far described shares several formal features with other rituals of purification and expiation in Africa—for example, the contact between person and spirit which must be broken and offerings which establish a communication and moral obligation. Many of these involve an act of sacrifice. An analysis that explores these features is T. O. Beidelman's (1966) study of Nuer sacrifice. Evans-Pritchard himself suggested that at the core of sacrifice is first a symbolism of substitution (1956: 282), where the victim dies instead of the man, and second, a transference onto the victim of that part of the self which is impure. Through sacrifice, the donor of the victim reorders his moral status. I bring up the comparison because there is some sort of identification between person and fowl in the Odieng ritual and because in the widow's ritual, which I describe in a later chapter, the notion of an externalization of self becomes explicit. Here I would suggest only a few brief and negative correspondences. Ehing do not, to my knowledge, have any identification with fowl outside the context of the ritual at Odieng, and this identification seems to be based only on the sexing of blood. Further, when Ehing sacrifice animals to a spirit, they drip its blood directly on the shrine, so that the spirit may receive its soul. No such offering occurs here, and though the priest ultimately eats the fowl, this in itself does not seem to warrant calling the fowl's death a sacrifice in the accepted religious meaning of that term. Finally, to my knowledge, Ehing do not think of the bird as a scapegoat.

6. One might, therefore, also suggest that the image of redness is not only the tabooed object but also a kind of report of the internal affliction. We will later see that, less literally, cadavers are also associated with blood loss; they are "dry." And if the "king" is not bloody, he is associated with fire and he wears red.

7. I wrote this passage before I learned, with great sorrow, that Sisa Sagna died in the summer of 1986. His loss will be felt by many.

Chapter 3: The Locality of Men

1. At the same time, persons within a House are aware of genealogical proximity. Ehing say that persons with a common paternal grandfather are of "one breast." This idiom, however, is rarely heard in everyday discourse.

2. There are two important normative corollaries of the ancestral charter in land. One implication of the idea that land is vested in a descent group is that no member of the House can permanently alienate his fields. He has exclusive rights to his plots throughout his life and will pass these rights to his children, but he cannot allocate land permanently to anyone not of his House. The other implication of land tenure is that, should the membership of a House be diminished, its members still retain jural control over all of the group's land, even though they could not possibly cultivate the amount of land under their control. In practice, however, they may lend the land to others on a temporary basis.

Chapter 4: The Movement of Women

1. Today, among the Ehing as well as throughout the Casamance, many youth are absent from the villages during the dry season. Consequently, much of marital tradition is no longer practiced. But the message of the marriage tale—that it is taboo for a woman to give birth in her own house—is still enforced with great tenacity. A woman, and especially a pregnant woman, must "walk."

When, as is sometimes the case, a woman returns from Dakar or from Ziguinchor pregnant, elders take immediate steps to observe the marriage rule. If a woman's lover is an Ehing youth, she will be escorted to his house before the time of delivery. But when her lover is a stranger, a youth whom she met in the towns and who lives elsewhere, her situation can lead to strained and awkward arrangements. As long as she stays in the village and does not leave to give birth outside the society, she must find a house into which to move. An acquaintance of mine was on the receiving end of one of these situations. He awoke one day to find a former friend, but never a lover, at his house to be his wife. My friend's father, at the solicitation of the girl's parents and without his knowledge, had given them wine for their daughter. When I asked the surprised husband why he had accepted the marriage, he replied that he could not shame his father by abrogating the arrangement. The marriage did not last long past the birth of the child.

2. It was Robert Hertz (1960) who, in his influential essay "Contribution to the Study of the Collective Representation of Death," advanced the idea that the fate of a corpse stood as a metaphor of fate of the soul. Hertz worked out his argument in the context of secondary burials in Indonesia, but his general insight has wide applicability. In the Ehing case, the treatment of the corpse does not point to any complex eschatological notions, for Ehing do not provide an elaborate description of the place where souls live under the fields; nor do they elaborate the journey from house to fields.

3. During one funeral, the procession stopped before reaching the grave and the body was taken to the side and hidden in the bush for an operation. The deceased was an old woman who had always had bad eyes; these were then being taken out so that when she returned she would not suffer from the same problem.

4. The elder who officiates stands in a *butaino* relationship. *Butaino,* as I remarked in the description of the harvest rite in the last chapter, are members of a House who inherit land when another House is extinguished. After striking down with the hatchet or the weaving knife and the other instruments associated with male and female work, the *butaino* takes these home. Several months later, the

children of the deceased offer the officiant a prestation of wine to reclaim the tools: the hatchet and knife, or the weaving knife and the cotton spinning tool. In the context of the social relationship, the meaning of this reclamation is not difficult to see: the tools stand for the land. When the *butaino* takes them home, he is pressing a claim and acting as if the death of an individual were the death of the House. In reclaiming the tools, the children deny the implications of this action. They reclaim the objects to work on the land of their parent.

Chapter 5: Initiation

1. There is a legend which states that Ehing discovered Kombutsu from a mole, which, according to Ehing, has a penis that looks as if it had been circumcised.

2. I might add here some sketchy information about the spirit Kaba which, though it will not resolve the question about Bunoken, may place it in a more comprehensive context. Kaba is a spirit known as the "wife" of Odieng, because the wife of the elder responsible to Odieng's shrine is responsible to Kaba. There is only one shrine of Kaba, located in Bakunum, but I was never allowed to attend any of the ceremonies there. All of the women of Ehing society gather at Kaba at least once a year and, with a libation, sacrifice a bull. Interestingly, men from the House in charge of Odieng come to this ceremony, but only, I was told, because they are necessary to kill the animal. I was told that women who have given birth for the first time in the previous year drink a mixture of wine with the bull's blood (and not the blood of an ox). Married women who have not yet given birth are offered a mixture of wine and sand, a symbolism whose implications I have already discussed.

3. Although there are no dances, the deceased was still questioned on his stretcher and sacrifices were made. An initiate who dies in the forest is not similarly treated but is secretly placed in the bush. By contrast, I was told that a woman who dies during childbirth would be given a public funeral.

Chapter 6: Widows

1. Perhaps one reason the second visit follows several months after the first is to be certain that the widow is not pregnant. If Odieng is distinguishing blood to avoid an ambiguity about fatherhood, a delay before the widow returns to a sexual life makes sense.

2. Of 66 men at Bakunum, 26 have been divorced at least once. Forty of the total 132 marriages of these men have ended in divorce.

Chapter 7: The Meaning of Rice

1. The youth usually put this money toward the activities of their recreation hall, especially toward dances. Each village association owns a stereo system that is run from car batteries.

2. In actuality, the amount of land needed by a family is a much more complex proposition. Yield depends on type of land, season, variety of seed, and so on.

Families, in turn, may eat well or conservatively, and may be small or large. One family I knew habitually ate one and one-half kilograms daily; another family, three. By the statement in the text, I intend only to give an indication of need.

3. Unlike the Moslems, who are a vast majority in Senegal, Ehing do not maintain that one must eat only with the right hand.

4. The "fictive" brother calls for an introductory note. When a woman reaches marriageable age, she enters into a relationship with a man who is of her patronym but not of her House. In that relationship, which is called "carrying wine" (*kapem buno*), the woman and man call each other *apima bunodze*, literally, "the carrier of my wine"; they also address each other by the term used between siblings of the opposite sex, *adinindze*. During the initial stages of the relationship, the man offers the woman gifts of wine, especially when she has need to visit a spirit. In return, he occasionally may receive a loincloth. As her "brother," he also receives one gourd of wine during the prestations for his sister's hand in marriage. Once a woman has given birth for the first time, the relevant feature of the relationship emerges. The brother instructs his wife to give a gift of his rice and salt to his sister with which to feed the latter's baby. This gift is said to establish the relationship with the woman's child, and with any children born later.

5. I once saw a sister's child take a wooden handle for a hatchet which his mother's brother (of the same age) had just completed.

6. Perhaps few single customs have been made to bear such theoretical weight as that of "ritual stealing." Jack Goody has provided an important review of this problem in 1959 and in later essays: "In African societies, a man in an agnatic system is prohibited from inheriting or succeeding to the property and office of his mother's descent or sibling group; the woman herself can exercise no rights, but her son often possesses what I have called residual claim through her which is given concrete expression in customs such as the snatching of goods belonging to the maternal uncle and other members of her lineage" (Goody 1973: 42). However, although Ehing are an "agnatic system," women do exercise rights in land. Both her male and female children still possess claims to goods, and these claims are held reciprocally by members of the mother's House.

7. This idea, in turn, owes much to Leach (1961) who noted that descent is often symbolized through notions of common substance and affinity through notions of mystical influence.

Chapter 8: Women and Land

1. For an account of land tenure among the neighboring Banjal-Diola, see Snyder (1981).

2. For a statement on the role of "sister" in patrilineal societies in Africa, see Sacks (1982).

Chapter 9: The Absent King

1. Some Ehing very vaguely alluded to the existence of a second king who once was an inhabitant of Etafun. Perhaps this marriage echoes this piece of possible history.

2. However, Thomas (1966: 14) relates that when a Fulup (Diola) *oei* died, they said "the earth is broken."

3. There is a weed called "fire" (*teno*) that also kills rice.

4. Leprosy is also associated with hyenas. Though Ehing said it was *munyo*, prohibited, to kill hyenas, they sometimes would do so when these animals attacked their stock. A hyena either killed or found dead was given a funeral, and its dried meat was given to lepers to treat the disease. For a structuralist analysis of the relations among leprosy, hyenas, and blacksmiths among the Kujamaat Diola, see Sapir (1981).

Chapter 10: The Hatchet's Fall

1. This image echoes that of the "rising knife" which announced Kombutsu. In 1690, a Portuguese priest described a similar image among a Manjaco people, several hundred miles south of the Ehing. A piece of iron, looking like the point of a knife, came out of the ground bit by bit near a shrine. It was only visible to an elder and was associated with the plentitude or scarcity of rice (Díaz 1945: 165). I thank Eric Gable for bringing this Manjaco practice to my attention.

2. The location is curious, for no shrine of Odieng is found in Kuguo today. Kuguo, once a thriving village, is now the site of only two or three houses. I would point out that, even though the grand shrine is on Nyame's land, its location—out in the woods—is in the general direction of Kuguo. Perhaps that is why the story locates the spirit there.

3. In the alternative version, is the cord that wraps Odieng umbilical? The image may well be polyvalent and symbolize the initiation as well. Men are also cut, and to announce the initiation, we recall, Ehing say "the fan-palm leaf has fallen."

4. For a phrasing of this issue, see Tsing and Yanagisako (1983: 511).

5. In his book, *Sacrifice in Africa,* Luc de Heusch (1985: 18) describes the Nuer concept of Kwoth in terms that formally fit Odieng as well. De Heusch traces the intervention of Kwoth in human affairs in relation to the notion of "respect" and prohibition. There are rules that forbid eating before in-laws, drinking water after burials, milking cattle during menstruation, contacting spoons of parents, sleeping with a nursing mother. Making a general interpretation, de Heusch notes that in defining these rules of separation, "The category *thek* functions like an operator, selecting a certain number of relations of symbolic incompatibility. As a classificatory system it constitutes, along with kinship rules, the symbolic foundation of all social structure."

Bibliography

Achebe, Chinua. *Things Fall Apart*. London: Heinemann, 1958.

Ardener, E. Review of *Purity and Danger*. *Man* (n.s.) 2 (1967): 139.

Beidelman, T. O. "The Ox and Nuer Sacrifice: Some Freudian Hypotheses about Nuer Symbolism." *Man* (n.s.) 1 (1966): 453–67.

———. "Swazi Royal Ritual." *Africa* 36 (1966): 373–405.

———. "Nuer Priests and Prophets: Charisma, Authority, and Power among the Nuer." In *The Translation of Culture*. Edited by T. O. Beidelman. London: Tavistock, 1971.

Bisilliat, Jeanne. "The Feminine Sphere in the Institutions of the Songhay-Zarma." In *Female and Male in West Africa*. Edited by C. Oppong. London: George Allen and Unwin, 1983.

Bohannan, L. and P. *The Tiv of Central Nigeria*. London: International African Institute, 1953.

da Cunha Taborda, Antonio. "Apontamentos etnograficos sobre os Felupes de Susana." *Boletin cultural da Guine Portuguesa* 5 (1950): 187–223; 511–60.

de Heusch, Luc. "The Debt of the Maternal Uncle: A Contribution to the Study of Complex Structures of Kinship." *Man* 9 (1974): 609–19.

———. *Sacrifice in Africa*. Bloomington: Indiana University Press, 1985.

Díaz, Antonio J., trans. "Grencas e costumes dos Indijenas da Ilha de Bissau," by Fr. Francisco Santiago. *Portugal em Africa*, 2d ser., II, No. 9 (1945).

Douglas Mary. *Purity and Danger*. London: Routledge and Kegan Paul, 1966.

171

Durkheim, Emile. *The Elementary Forms of the Religious Life.* New York: Free Press, 1915.

Evans-Pritchard, E. E. *Nuer Religion.* Oxford: Clarendon Press, 1956.

———. "The Divine Kingship of the Shilluk." In *Social Anthropology.* New York: The Free Press, 1962.

Fortes, Meyer. *The Dynamics of Clanship among the Tallensi.* London: Oxford University Press, 1945.

———. *The Web of Kinship Among the Tallensi.* London: Oxford University Press, 1949.

Girard, Jean. *Genèse du Pouvoir Charismatique en Basse Casamance.* Dakar, 1969.

Goody, J. "The Mother's Brother and the Sister's Son in West Africa." *Journal of the Royal Anthropological Society,* 89 (1959): 61–88.

———. "Bridewealth and Dowry in Africa and Eurasia." In *Bridewealth and Dowry* (see also essay by Stanley J. Tambiah). Cambridge: Cambridge University Press, 1973.

Griaule, Marcel. *Conversations with Ogotemmeli.* New York: Oxford University Press, 1965.

Guyer, Jane I. "Naturalism in Models of African Production." *Man* (n.s.) 19 (1984): 371–88.

Hertz, Robert. *Death and the Right Hand.* Translated by R. and C. Needham. New York: Free Press, 1960.

Jackson, Michael. *The Kuranko.* New York: St. Martin's Press, 1977.

Leach, E. R. *Rethinking Anthropology.* London: Athlone Press, 1961.

———. "Animal Categories and Verbal Abuse." In *Reader in Comparative Religion.* Edited by Lessa and Vogt. New York: Harper & Row, 1979 (1964).

———. *Social Anthropology.* New York: Oxford University Press, 1982.

Le Prince, J. "Les Bayottes." *A Travers le Monde* 41 (1905): 313–16; 321–24.

Lévi-Strauss, Claude. *The Savage Mind.* Chicago: University of Chicago Press, 1966.

———. "The Story of Asdiwal." In *The Structural Study of Myth and Totemism.* Edited by E. Leach. London: Tavistock, 1966.

Lienhardt, Godfrey. *Divinity and Experience.* Oxford: Oxford University Press, 1961.

Linares, Olga. "Agriculture and Diola Society." In *African Food Production Systems.* Edited by P. McLoughlin. Baltimore: Johns Hopkins University Press, 1970.

———. "Shell Middens of Lower Casamance and Problems of Diola Protohistory." *West African Journal of Archaeology,* 1 (1971): 23–54.

———. "From Tidal Swamp to Inland Valley: On the Social Organization of Wet Rice Cultivation among the Diola of Senegal." *Africa,* 51 (1981): 557–94.

Malinowski, Bronislaw. *Magic, Science, and Religion.* New York: Anchor Books, 1954.

Mark, Peter. *A Cultural, Economic, and Religious History of the Basse-Casamance Since 1500.* Stuttgart: Franz Steiner Verlag Wiesbaden, 1985.

Moore, Sally Falk. "Descent and Legal Position." In *Law in Culture and Society.* Edited by Laura Nader. Chicago: Aldine, 1969.

Needham, Rodney. *Reconnaissances*. Toronto: University of Toronto Press, 1980.

Netting, Robert Mc. *Hill Farmers of Nigeria*. Seattle: University of Washington Press, 1968.

Pélissier, Paul. *Les paysans du Senegal*. Saint-Yrieix (Haute-Vienne): Imprimerie Fabreque, 1966.

Portères, R. "Berceaux Agricoles Primaires sur le Continent Africain." *Journal of African History* 3 (1962): 195–210.

Radcliffe-Brown, A. R. *Structure and Function in Primitive Society*. New York: The Free Press, 1952.

Roche, Christian. *Conquête et résistance des peuples de Casamance*. Dakar: Les Nouvelles Editions Africaines, 1976.

Rodney, Walter. *A History of the Upper Guinea Coast*. New York: Monthly Review Press, 1970.

Sacks, Karen. *Sisters and Wives*. Urbana: University of Illinois Press, 1982.

Sahlins, Marshall. *Culture and Practical Reason*. Chicago: University of Chicago Press, 1976.

Sapir, J. David. "Kujaama: Symbolic Separation among the Diola-Fogny." *American Anthropologist* 72 (1970): 1330–48.

———. "Fecal Animals." *Man* (n.s.) 12 (1977): 1–21.

———. "Leper, Hyena, and Blacksmith in Kujumaat Diola Thought." *American Ethnologist* 8 (1981): 526–41.

Snyder, Francis. *Capitalism and Legal Change*. New York: Academic Press, 1981.

Southall, Aidan. "The Illusion of Nath Agnation." *Ethnology* 25 (1986): 1–20.

Steiner, Franz. *Taboo*. New York: Philosophical Library, 1956.

Thomas, L. V. *Les Diola*. Dakar, 1958/59.

———. "Bukut Chez les Diola-Niomoun." *Notes Africaines* 111 (1965).

———. "Initiation à la royauté chex les Floup." *Notes Africaines* 109 (1966): 10–19.

Tsing A., and S. Yanagisako. "Feminism and Kinship Theory." *Current Anthropology* 24 (1983): 511–16.

Turner, Victor. *The Drums of Affliction*. Ithaca: Cornell University Press, 1968.

Index

performance, 65–66; songs, 78–79; suspension of other spirits' powers, 65, 69; termination at Odieng, 88–90; transmission of sexual knowledge, 78, 87, 91, 93–94; trauma of, 75; "wrestling the heron," 73–74, 75, 93, 94
Intestines, 7, 53
Iri, as God, sky, rain, and year, 15

Jackson, Michael, 159

Kaba spirit, 168 (chap. 5, n. 2)
Kahin (lineage spirit): affliction by, 40; description and location of shrines, 39, 40; and group identity, 40; as marker of House and land, 39, 41–45, 46, 63; and prayers to ancestors, 40–41; role in funerals, 60; role in initiation, 69, 73; role in harvest ritual, 47–48; role in marriage ritual, 51–52
Kahus spirit, 69, 70, 76–77, 87
Kai spirit, 16, 148. See also Ai
Kin, uterine: identification of, 126–27; idiom of "possession," 127; rights and obligations of 127–31; role in funerals, 57, 61, 62
King. See Ai
Knife: in Kombutsu, 65; image of rising knife, 170n. 1
Kofyar, land rights among, 142–43
Kujamaat-Diola: food taboos of, 123–24; widow's rite, 103
Kuranko, 159

Land: anomaly in inheritance, 10–11, 110; categories, 115–16; as claimed by lineage founders, 12–13; disputes, 133, 140; Ehing attachment to, 133–34; of extinguished Houses, 46; as property of house, 41–45, 46, 63; as source of souls, 63, 134. See also Rice fields
Leach, Edmund, 5, 6
Leprosy, 150, 170 (chap. 9, n. 4)
Lévi-Strauss, Claude, 124, 157
Linares, Olga, ix, xi, 13, 111, 115, 117
Locality of men: as idiom of descent, 10, 41, 63; in marriage myth, 33–34

Malinowski, Bronislaw, 34
Mandinka, xiii
Manjaco, 146
Mark, Peter, xi
Marriage: cross-cousin marriage, 55; interpretation of myth, 33–34, 63; marrige payments, 50; marriage proscriptions, 54–55; marriage ritual, "Holding Out

the Spoon," 50–52; movement of women in, 9–10, 47; myth of origin, 9, 31–33; relation to cycle of souls, 10; role of intermediary in arrangement of marriage, 50
Meander: as boundary of village, 111; as symbol in funeral ritual, 62
Menstrual taboos, 4, 54
Moore, Sally Falk, 39
Mosquitoes, 112, 165n. 2
Mothers: feeding of infants, 124; ritual of Ibun, 124–25
Munyo (taboo), xiv–xv, 24
Myth, as social theory, 35, 158

Names: changes at death, 97; cycling through generations, 63
Ndembu, 26–27
Needham, Rodney, 130
Netting, Robert Mc., 142
Nuer: concept of Kwoth, 158, 159, 170n. 5; concept of sacrifice, 166n. 5
Nyassia, xii

Odieng (Hatchet spirit): activity in contrast to Ndembu spirits, 26; affliction, 3, 12, 17, 25; casting off taboos in ritual, 21–23; curing ritual at, 18–23; and governing of production and reproduction, 5, 10, 160; group life, not connected with problems of, 26; initiation ritual, 88–90; as instrument of classification, 159–60; medicine of Odieng, 166n. 4; as moral agent, 17, 22; myth of arrival, 153–56; privacy of ritual, 25–26; rules (prohibitions) of, 4–5, 22; rules as conceptual system, 27; shrines, 16, 23–24; how symbolism works, 22–23; widow's ritual at, 98, 100–3
Odieng Iri (Hatchet of the Sky), 152–53

Palm trees, ix
Palm wine: in funeral, 57, 58; in marriage, xiii, 50; in Odieng's rules, 4, 145; and seasons, xiii; as symbol of men's work, 130–31; tapping as men's work, xii
Patronyms (and patronymic categories), 14–15, 54
Pélissier, 13, 111, 118
Portères, R., ix
Pregnancy: "covering" from men, 53; rite (Bufine), 52–53; in unmarried women, 167n. 1
Procreation, Ehing view of, 52
Prohibition, theories of, 5–9. See also Food taboos; Menstrual taboos; Munyo

Rain, 15, 34, 111, 112, 142, 148–49, 157
Rain-priest. *See* Ai
Reincarnation. *See* Cycle of Souls
Residence. *See* Locality
Rice: in contrast to wine, 131; domestication in Casamance, ix; in funerals, 57, 58; as gift of uterine kin, 130; men's and women's to feed family, 119–20, 143; as symbol of female work, 10, 143; as symbol of women's productive powers, 130, 131, 132, 143–44; and wealth, 118–19; yield, 117–18
Rice fields: division of fields, 135; ecological interpretations of inheritance, 141–43; jural interpretations of inheritance, 140–44; location, 115–16; measurement of male and female fields, 140; size of fields, 113; symbolic interpretations of inheritance, 143–44; transmission to women, 137–39
Roche, Christian, xii
Rodney, Walter, ix
Rope ritual, 129

Salt, ritual use of, 106
Sapir, J. David, xi, 103, 123
Seasons, 112, 151, 160
Senghor, Leopold L., 25
Separation of sexes: defined through Odieng, 4–5, 131; and notions of sexual power, 132, 157, 160; as pivot of social structure, 4, 64, 109, 156. *See also* Contradiction
Shilluk, 150
Sky. *See* Iri
Soul: Ehing concept of, 48; loss as death, 56; stolen by witches, 59, 125. *See also* Cycle of Souls
Southall, Aidan, 157
Spirits: categories of, 15–16; idiom of catching, 17; shrines, 16. *See also* Bal-

iga; Echin; Kahin; Kahus; Kai; Odieng; Teno
Steiner, Franz, 94
Symbolic anthropology, 11

Taboo. *See* Prohibition
Tallensi, 11, 141
Teno (fire) spirit, 150
Termite hills: in initiation, 72; in "rope," 129
Thomas, Louis-Vincent, 65
Tiv, 11

Villages, 13

Warfare, 105
Weaving knife, 61–62, 100
Widow: as carrier of male blood, 102; moral ambiguity of, 99; period of mourning, 99–100; remarriage of, 103; restrictions on behavior, 99; visits to Odieng, 5, 100–4
Widower: contrast to widow, 98; rites of separation, 100
Witches, witchcraft: and changes of residence, 43; discussion of in funeral ritual, 58–60; "eating" souls, 59, 125; and explanations of death, 59–60; identification of, 125; jealousy as motive, 43–45, 118–19, 125; and the male initiation, 77, 81, 87; and mother's milk, 125; and notions of revenge, 59–60; and snakes, 60
Women: economic role of, 10, 113, 119, 130, 132; "giving birth" as notion of feminine power, 124, 132, 144

Youth/Elder distinction, 4, 53, 72, 87
Youtou, 105

Ziguinchor, 39, 52, 167
Zombie (*nyazango*), 62–63

About the Author

MARC R. SCHLOSS is a cultural anthropologist who received his Ph.D. from the University of Virginia. He has taught anthropology at Virginia, the University of South Carolina, Sweet Briar College, and Bucknell University. This book on the Ehing people draws from his twenty-two months of research in Senegal in the late 1970s.